HIRSCHFELD'S ICONS

a poster book

by DAVID LEOPOLD

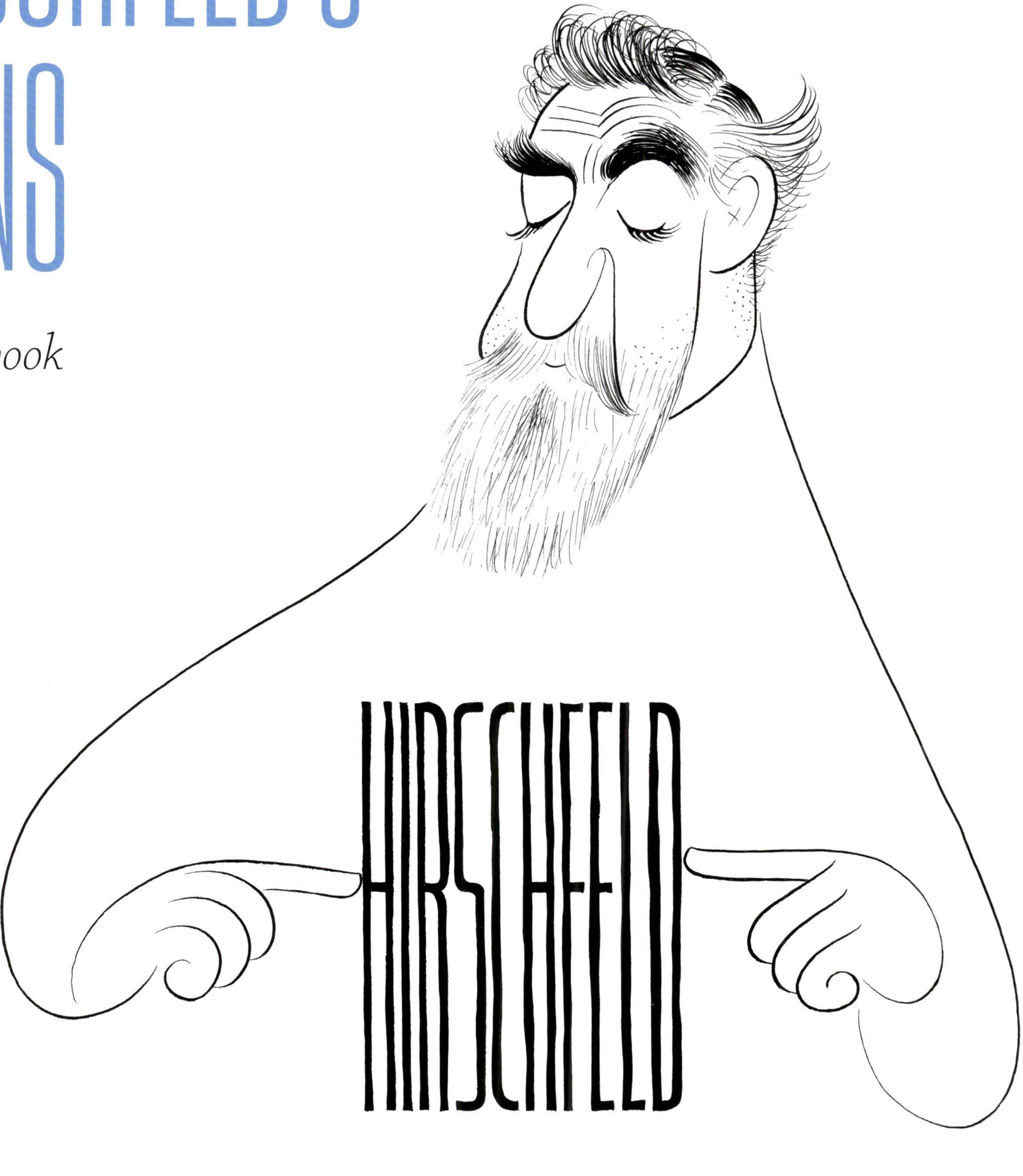

art by AL HIRSCHFELD

introduction by Dick Cavett

ABRAMS COMICARTS, NEW YORK

CONTENTS

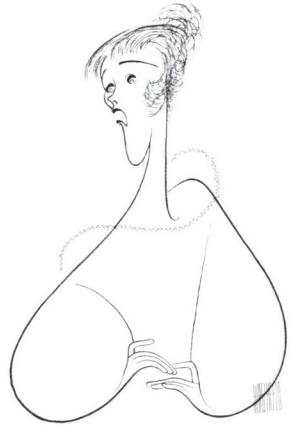

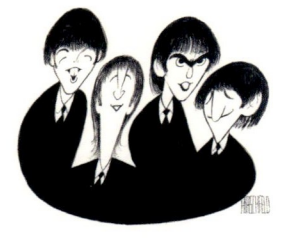

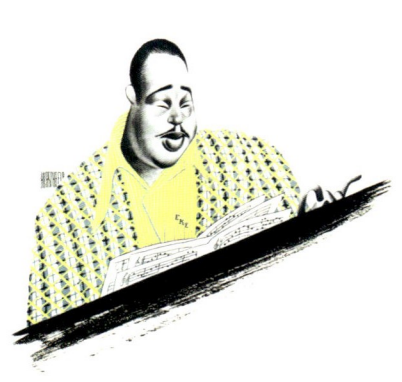

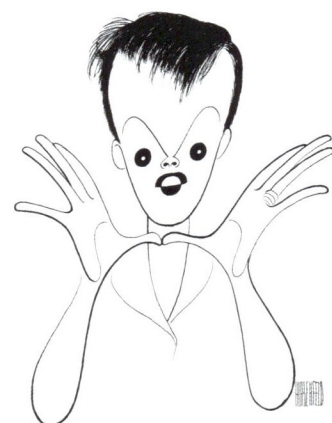

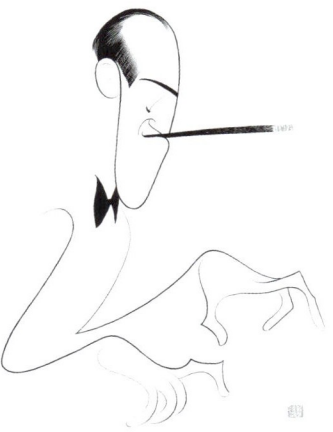

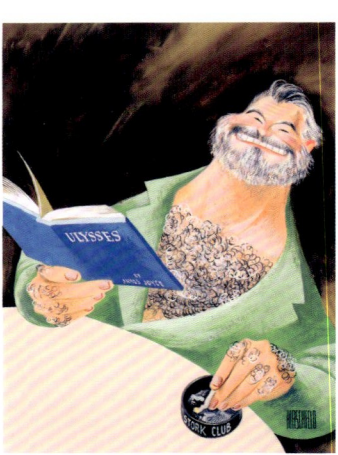

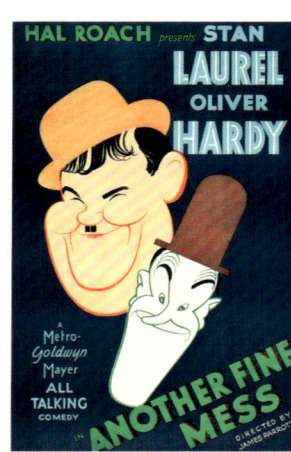

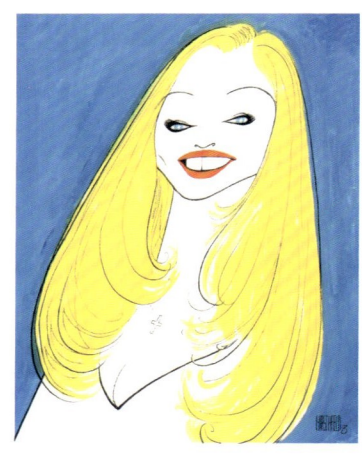

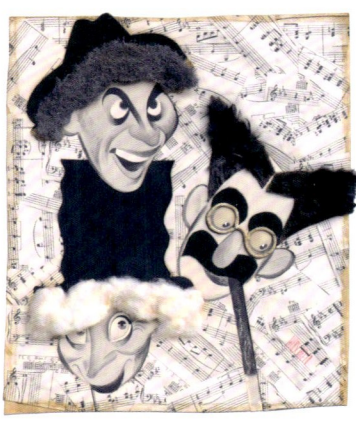

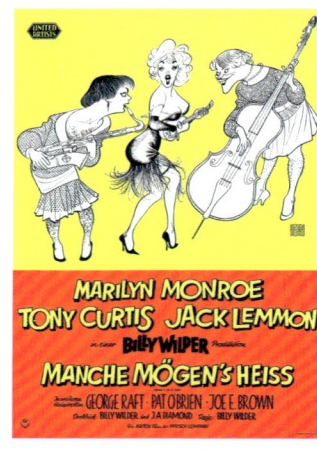

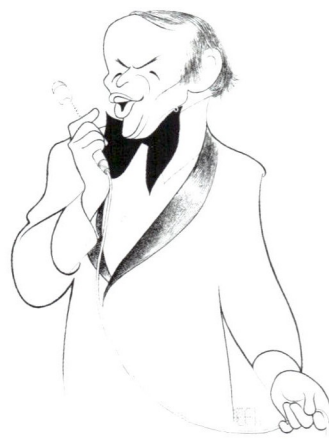

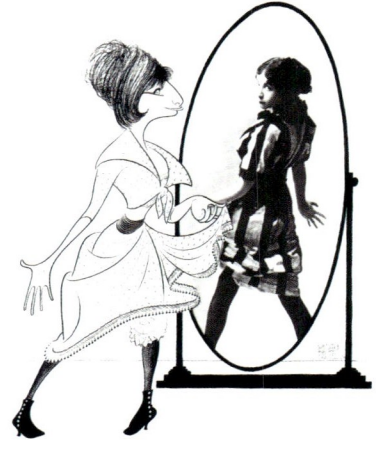

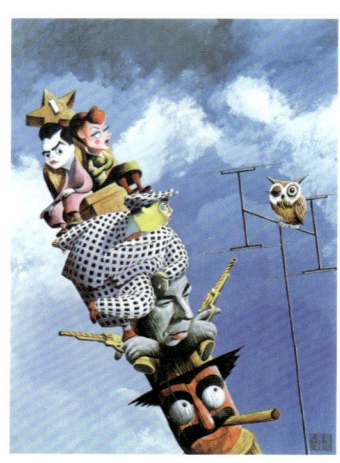

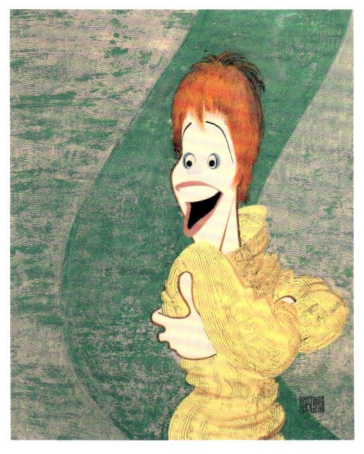

Carol Burnett

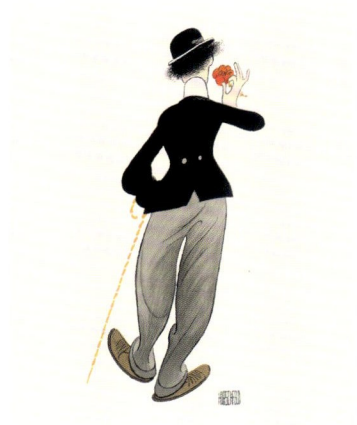

Charlie Chaplin

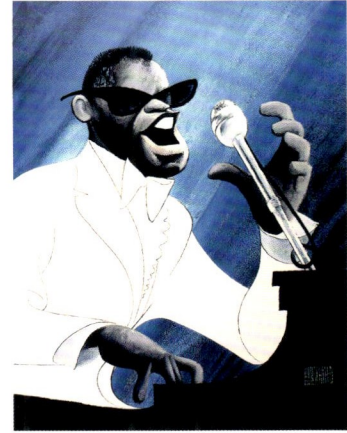

Ray Charles

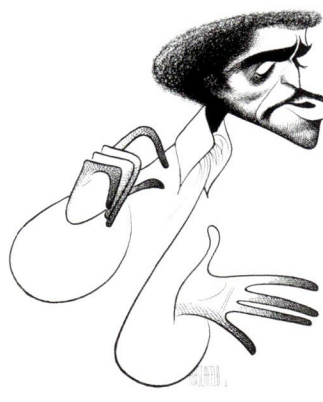

Sammy Davis Jr.

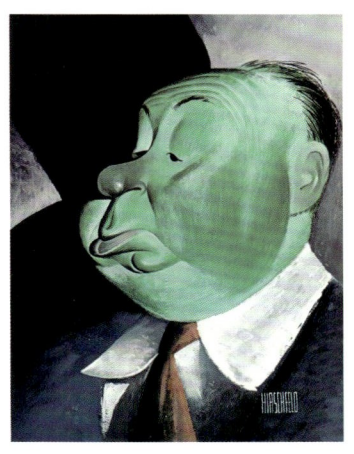

Alfred Hitchcock

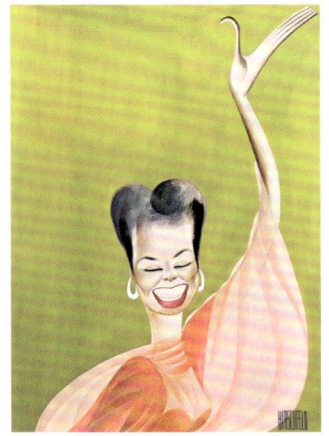

Lena Horne

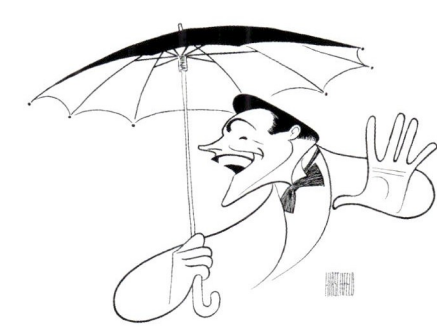

Gene Kelly

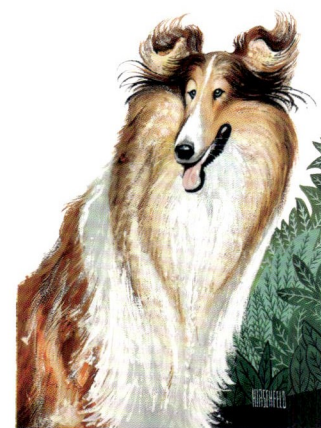

Lassie

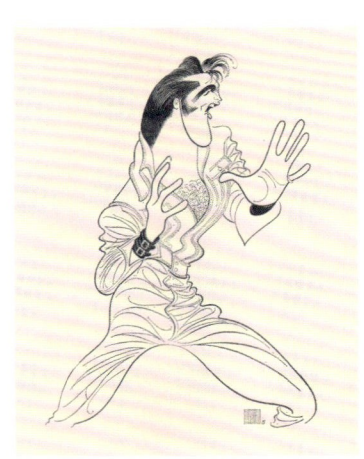

Elvis Presley

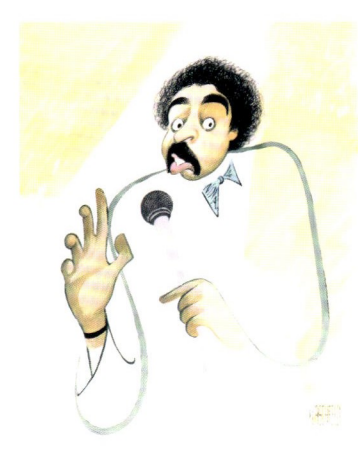

Richard Pryor

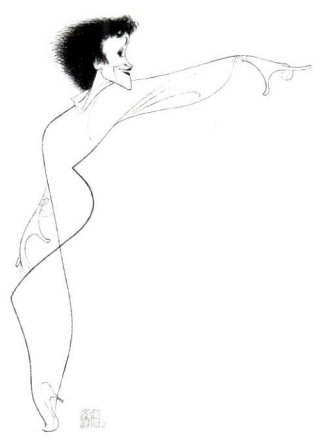

Chita Rivera

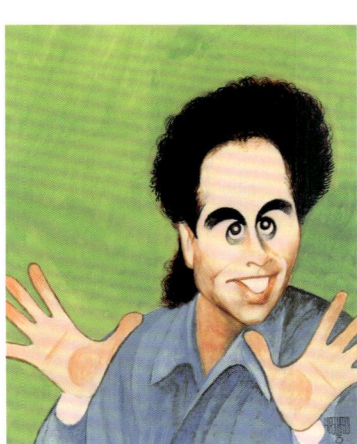

Jerry Seinfeld

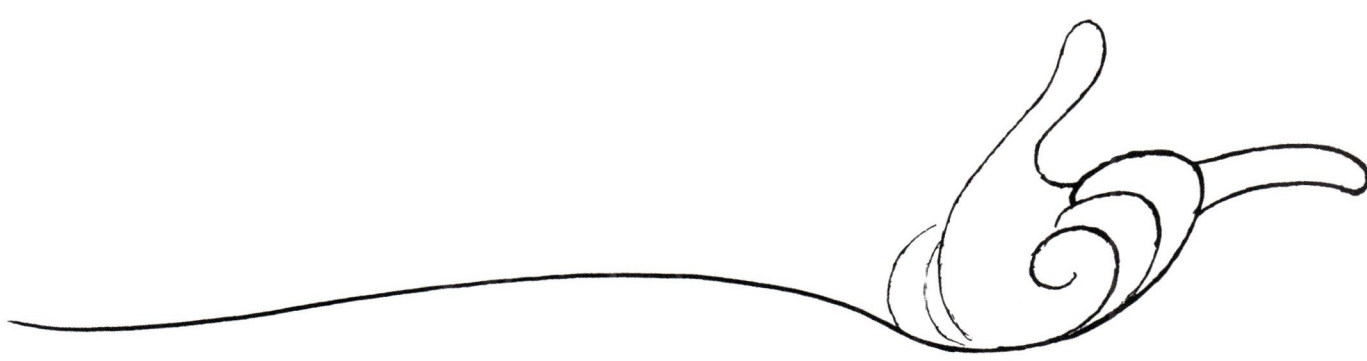

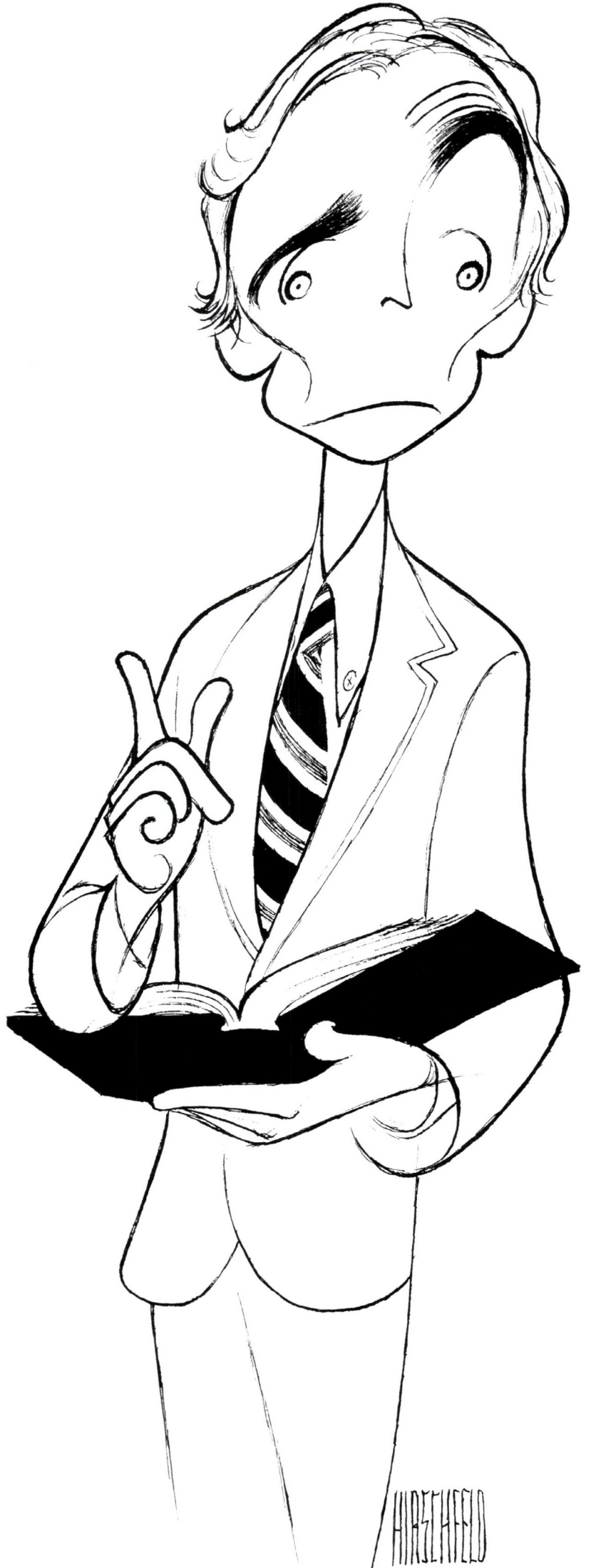

A PARADE OF HIRSCHFELD ICONS

by Dick Cavett

There was, once upon a considerably grander time in Manhattan, a man who could conjure magic with ink the way Fred Astaire could with his feet. Al Hirschfeld, with nib and flourish, gave us not mere caricatures, but the distilled quiddity of the greats. A line here, a curl there, and suddenly you were looking at Streisand or Groucho or Satchmo—not simply captured but *revealed*. Those lines—so few, yet so unmistakenly *them*—were like lightning that somehow sat still long enough to be framed.

I remember the sensation of opening the Sunday *New York Times* Arts & Leisure section and finding Hirschfeld's latest. Before I registered the Broadway review or the critic verdict, I looked for the drawing. I suspect half of New York did the same; if we could admit it, Hirschfeld *was* the review, with all apologies to all the Riches and Kerrs of this world. The show might have been heaven or dreck, but you knew it had lived, at least once, in Hirschfeld's hand.

Part of the suspense was the hunt. Ninas. (For those two or three of you who have been out of town since 1945: Hirschfeld hid his daughter's name in his drawings.) There you sat, squinting at Liza or Brando or Merman as rendered by a jazz riff of ink, counting the looping *N*s, delighted as if you'd discovered buried treasure. There are those who claim to have been late for curtain because they were lost in a futile search, and I believe them.

What was his sorcery? I've stared more at his work than I care to confess, wondering how a single line, unbroken, could do what a thousand brushstrokes never will. All the greats, rendered by Hirschfeld, sitting eternally still yet vibrating with life.

There is a happy contradiction at play: Hirschfeld was not in the business of flattery, yet his subjects prized being lampooned by him. It was the imprimatur of Broadway's gods, and it was done with a laugh. I can attest I never heard anyone say, "He made

LEFT
Dick Cavett in *Into the Woods*, 1988

OPPOSITE
Hirschfeld, Cavett, and Charles Addams
Dick Cavett surrounded by two icons of cartoon and caricature.
On the left, Al Hirschfeld, and the right, Charles Addams, c. 1970s

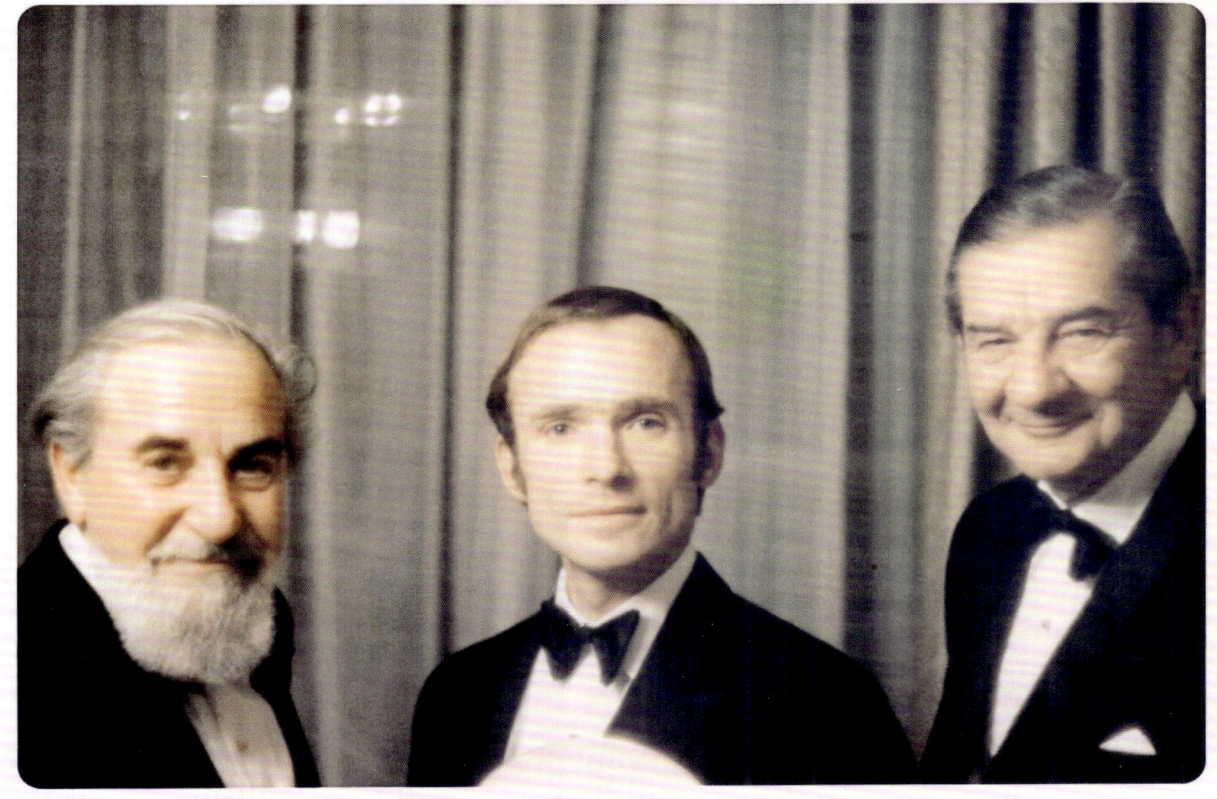

me look awful." They all smiled, sheepishly, proudly—even when he slyly exaggerated what nature had already hinted at.

And so, this book. A parade of Hirschfeld icons—frameable posters with erudite descriptions to remind or teach the reader what we need to know about these depicted giants. To gather them in one place is to gather much of the twentieth century's theatrical memory. If you squint long enough, it is a kind of American history. Yours to linger over, laugh with, and occasionally gasp at—as if you are again breathless in Row G, watching the lights dim, while a Hirschfeld sketch has somehow leapt from your program and onto the stage. These drawings are, to my eye, the closest ink has come to applause.

Now, it does seem a bit mad that this collection offers us only twenty-five icons. The man chronicled nearly a century of Broadway, Hollywood, television, politics, sports, and even opera. He drew presidents and professors and jazzmen, dancers and eccentrics, and legends by the battalion. Reduce that to twenty-five and you are, with my sympathy, committing triage on Mount Olympus. Hirschfeld belongs in every living room, dorm room, music room, den, locker, or local pub. To make these works accessible, affordable, and ready to hang is something of a cultural public service.

Speaking of service, I must confess a personal delight: I am among the faces in this collection. I suppose it's because I got to write this introduction, but my pedigree is genuine. I knew Al and had the honor of being his subject four times—the first in 1972 as part of a mural for Creative Management Associates; then, in 1988, when I appeared in Stephen Sondheim's *Into the Woods* (on the opposite page); a portrait from 1997 for my show *In Other Words . . . Dick Cavett*; and finally, in 2000, when I appeared as the narrator in a revival of *The Rocky Horror Show* on Broadway. Not bad for a kid from Nebraska.

To be Hirschfelded is to join a pantheon of scribbled immortals, drawn with the lightest touch and the deepest wit. I am not above admitting I will be framing them all, side by side—my betters and my equals, my idols and my fellow victims of Hirschfeld's benevolent, merciless pen.

So turn the page. Begin your own gallery. And save room on your bookshelf and walls for Volume Two, which I hope, for the sake of civilization, is already in production.

Dick Cavett
October 2025
Ridgefield, Connecticut

Dick Cavett has spent most of his life in front of some sort of audience—be it in a television studio, atop a Broadway stage, or, occasionally, next to his own fireplace reading Groucho Marx aloud to bewildered guests. After years playing a variety of starring roles in a variety of media, and as host of his eponymous television program, which featured more sparkling conversation than a dinner with Dorothy Parker and fewer fistfights than one with Norman Mailer, he took up writing essays for *The New York Times*, thereby achieving the dual metropolitan aim of sounding off and being published. He is a sometime actor, a sometime author, a frequent poster collector, an award winner, and one of the rare living beings to claim an Al Hirschfeld portrait that makes him look slightly taller than in real life. Cavett continues to marvel at the uncanny power of wit, words, and well-chosen company. He divides his time between a battered old desk in New York, less-battered chairs in Connecticut, and anywhere people are still thoughtful enough to laugh at the right things.

THE ICON BUSINESS

by David Leopold

An icon can be many things. History is full of religious icons—totems that have been venerated in churches, temples, and mosques. Anyone with a computer or smartphone understands that the icons on their screens are graphic representations of an action or application, and that emojis are distillations of emotions or ideas. The most effective of these feature only the most minimal characteristics, and yet they are accurate and undisputable. When it comes to popular culture, an icon is a personality so famous, their image is recognized by a majority of people. So, when it came to creating iconic images, it could be said that Al Hirschfeld was in the icon business.

For generations, Hirschfeld's drawings of performers and personalities provided iconic images that audiences instantly recognized—Carol Channing in *Hello, Dolly!*, Liza Minnelli in *Cabaret*, and Zero Mostel in *Fiddler on the Roof*, to name just a few. Hirschfeld loved drawing stage clowns and early silent film comedians because, as he observed, "they invented themselves. They were much easier to do, to establish a symbol for. Ed Wynn, Bert Lahr, the Marx Brothers, Fred Allen, Laurel and Hardy . . . all of these figures had one thing in common. Apart from their appetite for the theater, they looked like their caricatures. The caricature, with its immediacy and almost trademark quality, became the image the public figure was striving to become."

Performers understand this. They want to be remembered for this or that role, and they understood that Hirschfeld's drawings made it easier for audiences to remember them. You could consult the cast list of the original 1950 Broadway production of *Guys and Dolls* and might not know each of the actors by name, but looking at the Hirschfeld drawing of the show, you can immediately recognize them in their greatest roles.

Film studio and theater producers recognized the importance Hirschfeld could play in a production's viability. This is why Hirschfeld worked regularly for a half dozen studios, but perhaps most significantly with MGM, the biggest studio in the Golden Age of Hollywood in the 1930s and '40s, whose motto was "More stars than there are in heaven." MGM's impressive

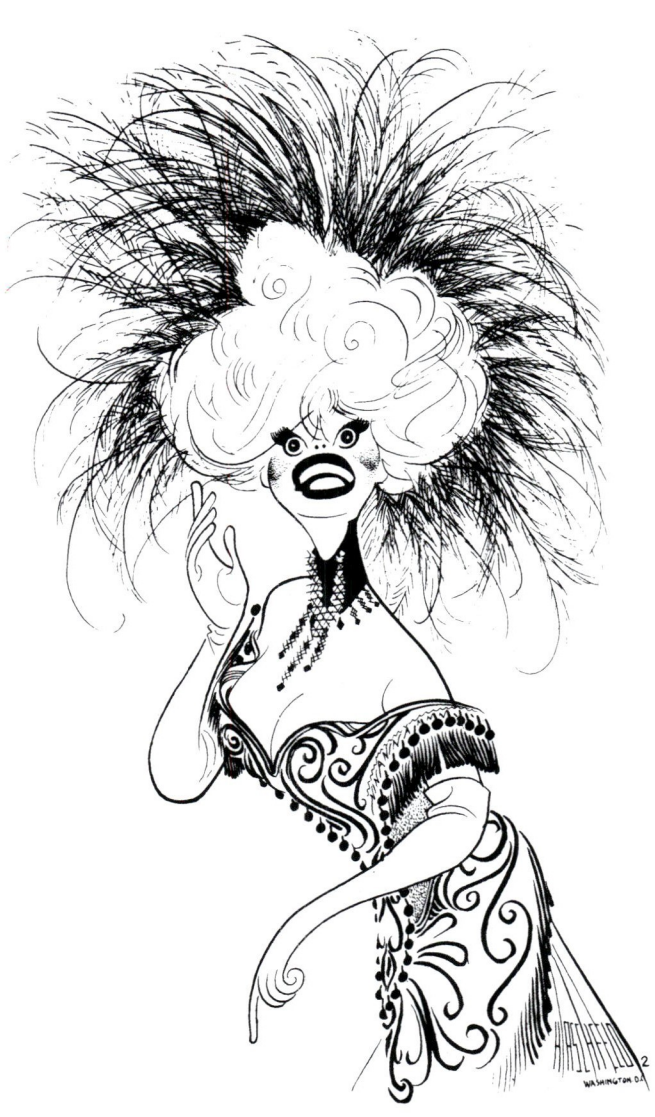

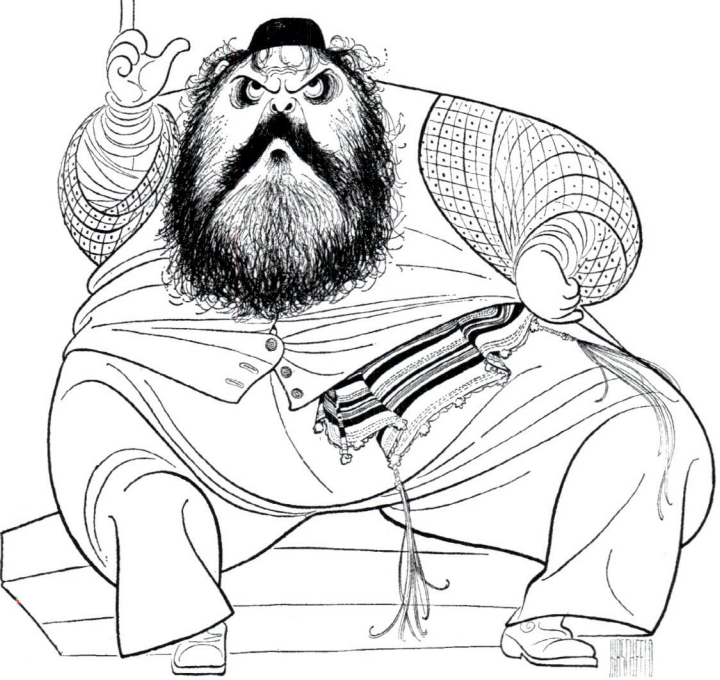

TOP
Carol Channing in *Hello, Dolly!*, 1964

RIGHT
Zero Mostel in *Fiddler on the Roof*, 1964

list of well-known performers was a perfect fit for Hirschfeld's natural ability to turn a personality into an icon everyone could identify. Broadway producers were also aware that Hirschfeld's legend-making imagery could help propel a show to success. That is why they hired him to draw more theater posters than any other artist, and why a handful of those have literally become the icon of the show, such as *My Fair Lady*, *Man of La Mancha*, and *Porgy and Bess*.

Even the federal government recognized Hirschfeld's unique ability to capture both the look and the character of an icon. In 1991, it issued the first US postage stamps ever to include an artist's name and signature, "Comedians by Hirschfeld." The five stamps included Abbott and Costello and Fanny Brice, and were followed in 1994 with ten stamps honoring the "Stars of the Silent Screen," which featured those performers Hirschfeld had made iconic seven decades earlier, such as Buster Keaton, Lon Chaney, and Charlie Chaplin.

Hirschfeld's ease in turning actor into avatar, and image into icon, over an eighty-two-year active career, did not make selecting the twenty-five icons featured in this poster book easy. There were simply too many to choose from. He drew all the heavyweights of the theater in his seventy-six years covering that beat primarily for New York newspapers. And he drew so many Oscar winners that when *The Line King*, a documentary about his life and career, was nominated for an Oscar in 1996, it seemed par for the course. No one contributed more *TV Guide* covers than Hirschfeld. His artwork was featured on more than 250 record album covers. And yet, many of the stars from Hirschfeld's nine-decade career don't hold a central place in our contemporary popular culture. Most people under the age of thirty-five would be hard pressed to identify Carol Channing, Marlene Dietrich, Spencer Tracy, or Ginger Rogers, let alone watch any of their performances. In fact, Hirschfeld captured the band Aerosmith in an iconic image for the cover of their album *Draw the Line* more than forty years ago—an image the band still uses. But will anyone have any idea who they are forty years from now? Cultural currency loses value quickly.

But icons . . . icons are forever. So as we sifted through the many considerations, we ended up with those who have stood the test of time and whose work still resonates with today's audiences, although cases could be made for at least another twenty-five or more performers. As award-winning playwright Terrence McNally recognized, "No one 'writes' more accurately

of the performing arts than Al Hirschfeld. He accomplishes on a blank page with his pen and ink in a few strokes what many of us need a lifetime of words to say." Even with the selections made, we had another formidable hurdle to clear. At the start of this poster book series, it was decided that we would not use any images that had been published as hand-signed limited-edition prints. Although the exquisite reproductions in this book have none of the collecting value of actual fine art, the Al Hirschfeld Foundation wanted to honor Hirschfeld's commitment to not publish competing images at varying price points. That said, there are two full-page poster images in this book that have been published as limited-edition signed prints: Looking through the twenty-three drawings Hirschfeld created of Marilyn Monroe, we felt that his image of her in *Some Like It Hot* was the most iconic portrait of her that he had created. After much palaver, we decided to use the German film poster that featured Hirschfeld's "cast" image, since the original black-and-white image had been

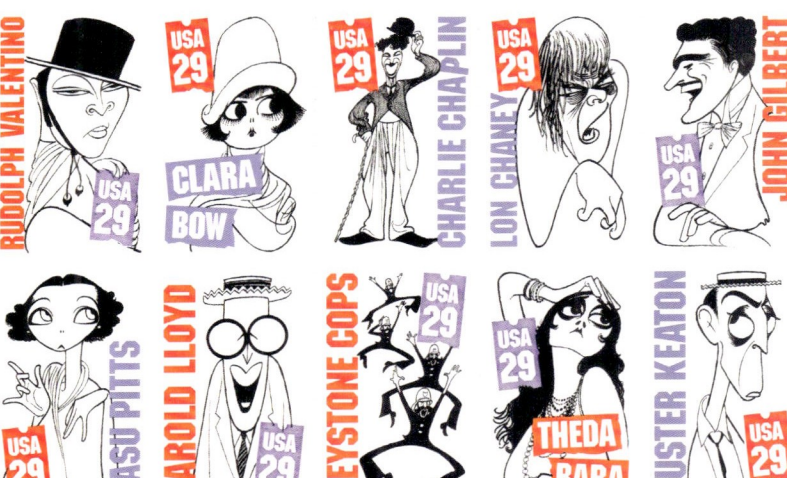

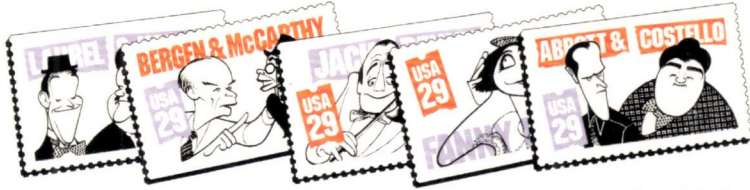

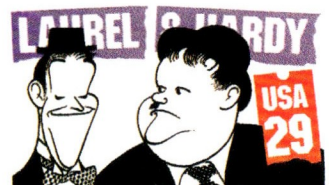
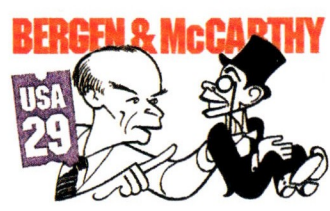
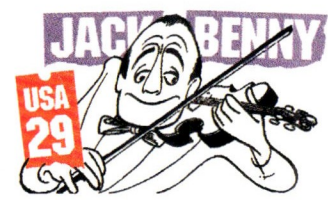
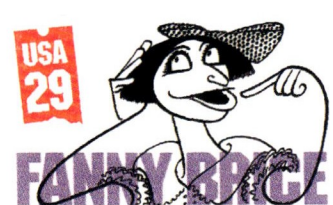
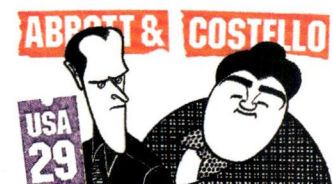

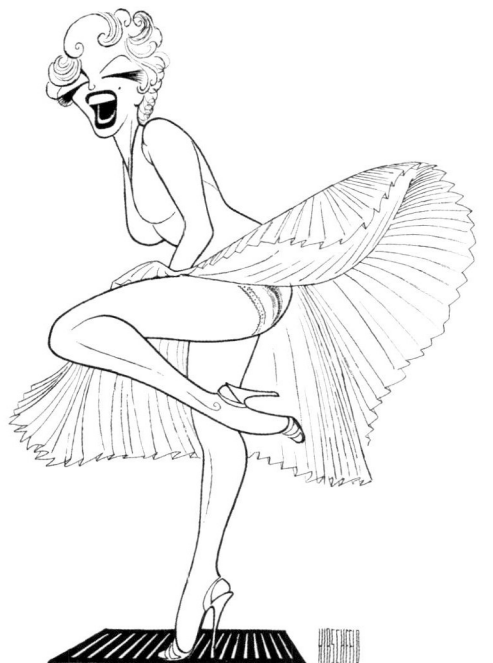

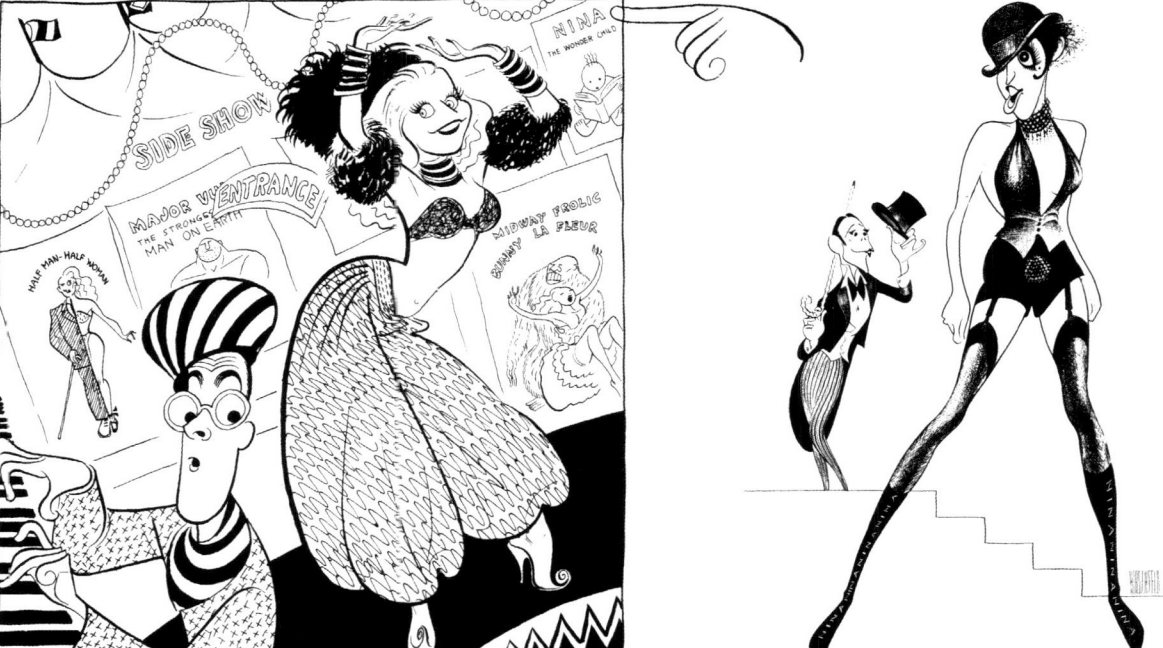

published as a print. The same is true for Elvis. Hirschfeld's legendary drawing of Elvis's "comeback" was so iconic that Hirschfeld returned to it on several occasions. We decided to present it here as it was originally seen by millions when it first ran as a newspaper illustration. Neither competes with its limited-edition signed counterpart.

When a performer is iconic, often they are so popular that a single name (first or last) is all that is required to know who is being talked about. This book has several: Elvis, Marilyn, Madonna, and Groucho. Even Laurel and Hardy, Chaplin, Sinatra, Streisand, and Hitchcock. But there is a one-name wonder who is iconic in Hirschfeld's work and present in almost every image in this book: Nina. Hirschfeld's daughter's name is the one most associated with his work other than his own. When Nina was born in 1945, the proud father snuck the letters of her name into a poster in the background of a drawing for the play *Are You With It?* In his next drawing, he found another place to hide her name. This "infantile prank," according to the artist, was meant for family and friends, and after a few more he stopped (even a good joke can overstay its welcome). But when Hirschfeld was deluged by mail after leaving her name out of a drawing for the Sunday *New York Times*, he decided it was easier to keep the name in than answer all the correspondence asking where the NINA was hidden. He tried to end the "national insanity" several more times over the years, but each time he got the

same result, only with larger piles of mail after each omission. He said he learned "the hard way" to put her name into his drawings before he put his own, as no one was looking for his name.

Fifteen years after he began hiding NINAs in his art, a *Times* reader wrote the paper extolling the virtues of Hirschfeld's drawings, but asking if it was possible to let readers know how *many* NINAs they should be looking for, as Hirschfeld was hiding them multiple times in his work (instances that, by this time, were being integrated organically as he drew). Hirschfeld's response—unheralded and unexplained at the time—was to simply put a number next to his signature to indicate how many NINAs to look for.

These NINAs have become such an integral part of Hirschfeld's work that when he submitted his sketches to the US Postal Service for the stamps, he was informed that there was a rule against hidden messages, so Hirschfeld omitted any NINAs. When the postmaster general first saw the final art, he stared at it for some time before asking the art director where the NINAs were. When reminded of the rule, the postmaster general said that they really weren't Hirschfeld drawings unless they had NINAs. The art director sheepishly returned the drawings to the artist and asked if he could insert any into the designs. Hirschfeld did his best, but some had no place for a NINA and therefore do not have them, giving those icons one more thing that makes them special.

But to be drawn by Hirschfeld *was* special. Critic Brendan Gill wrote, "To be a star on Broadway is to have one's name in lights, yes, but it is also, and more significantly, to be drawn by Hirschfeld." Awards are nice, but for many performers, being captured in pen and ink by Hirschfeld was the ultimate honor. It meant they were part of a tradition; a portrait gallery that included some of the biggest names in popular culture. It also meant that they were immortalized—indelible as any tattoo and monumental as any statue. After all, more people saw Hirschfeld's drawing of a performance than those who saw the actual production itself.

Al Hirschfeld was himself an icon, recognized by performers and audiences. Clearly game recognizes game.

ABOVE, LEFT
Marilyn Monroe in *The Seven Year Itch*, 1983

ABOVE, MIDDLE
Are You With It?, 1945
LEFT TO RIGHT: Johnny Downs and Joan Roberts, 1945
This was the first drawing to feature a hidden NINA (top right).

ABOVE, RIGHT
Liza Minnelli and Joel Grey in *Cabaret*, 1972

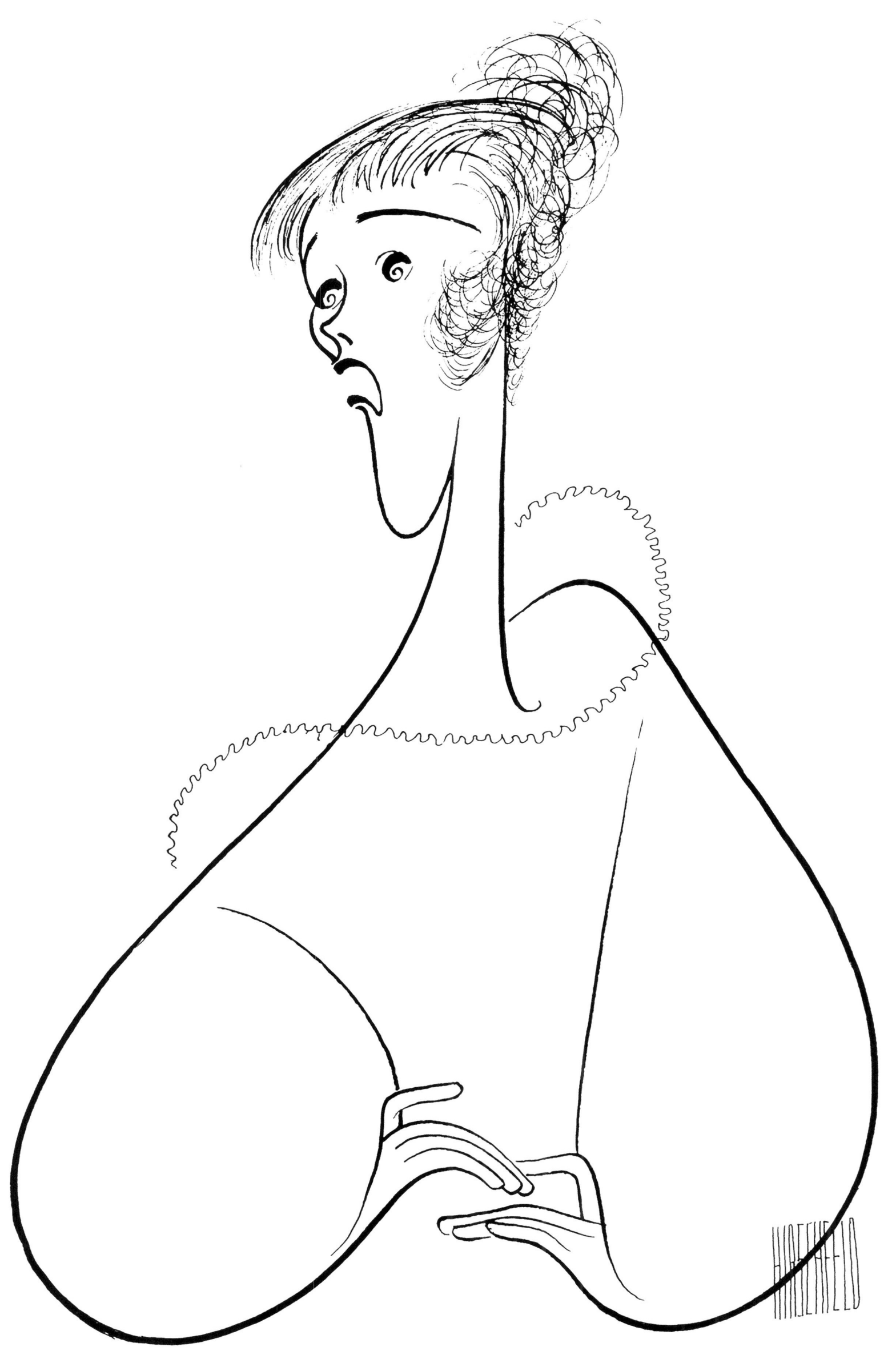

JULIE ANDREWS

b. October 1, 1935

Ink on board, 1977

The New York Times, August 21, 1977

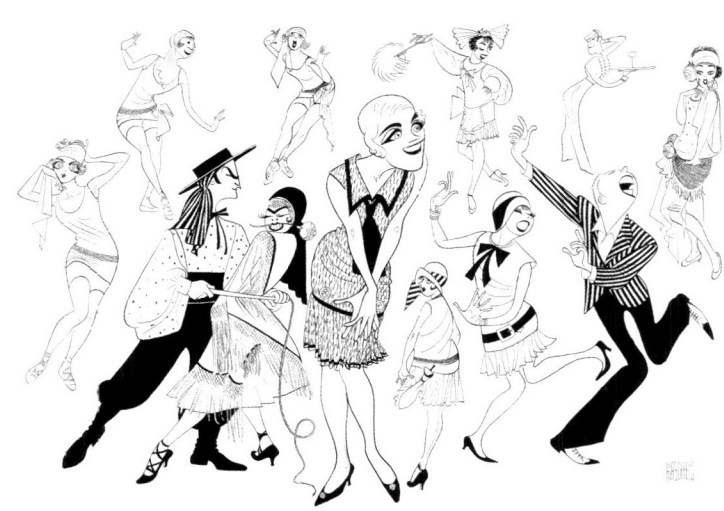

Julie Andrews entered the American public's consciousness in 1954 when she became a star on Broadway in *The Boy Friend*, a musical set in the 1920s, and has maintained icon status ever since. Hirschfeld marked Andrews's arrival with a drawing celebrating her one hundredth performance in this show. Over the next forty-eight years, Hirschfeld would draw Andrews more than any other actress—from her stage successes in *My Fair Lady* and *Camelot* to her classic roles in films such as *The Sound of Music* and *Mary Poppins*.

In 1968, 20th Century-Fox was so convinced they had a blockbuster film in *Star!*, a biopic of actress and singer Gertrude Lawrence, that they literally spared no expense in promoting it. The press kit, made to look like a performer's traveling trunk, was filled with twenty-five Hirschfeld drawings of Andrews in the starring role. Unfortunately, the world was not ready for their beloved prim-and-proper legend to play a down-and-dirty, tough-as-nails music hall queen, and the film was a bomb. Andrews made two other films that flopped—*Darling Lili* and *The Tamarind Seed*—and her career seemed to stall.

This drawing captures Andrews at a moment of reinvention. After nursing her wounds in a chalet in Switzerland, she began to perform concerts again, with residencies in Las Vegas; Los Angeles; and Westchester, New York. Andrews would soon return to film and the theater, first appearing in an off-Broadway Stephen Sondheim revue (*Putting It Together* in 1993), and two years later on Broadway in a musical adaptation of *Victor/Victoria*, the hit 1983 film she starred in as a cross-dressing singer. For almost five decades, Hirschfeld captured it all. "When Hirschfeld drew a likeness of me, he always made my chin quite pronounced—even slack jawed," remembered Andrews. "This began, I believe, during the *My Fair Lady* years when my portrayal of Eliza, as a cockney girl, did have a somewhat slack-jawed air. And I guess the impression stuck! Some thirty or forty years later—by which time the chin had definitely filled out—Tony Walton tactfully suggested to Hirschfeld that he modify the likeness a bit and the dear man did!"

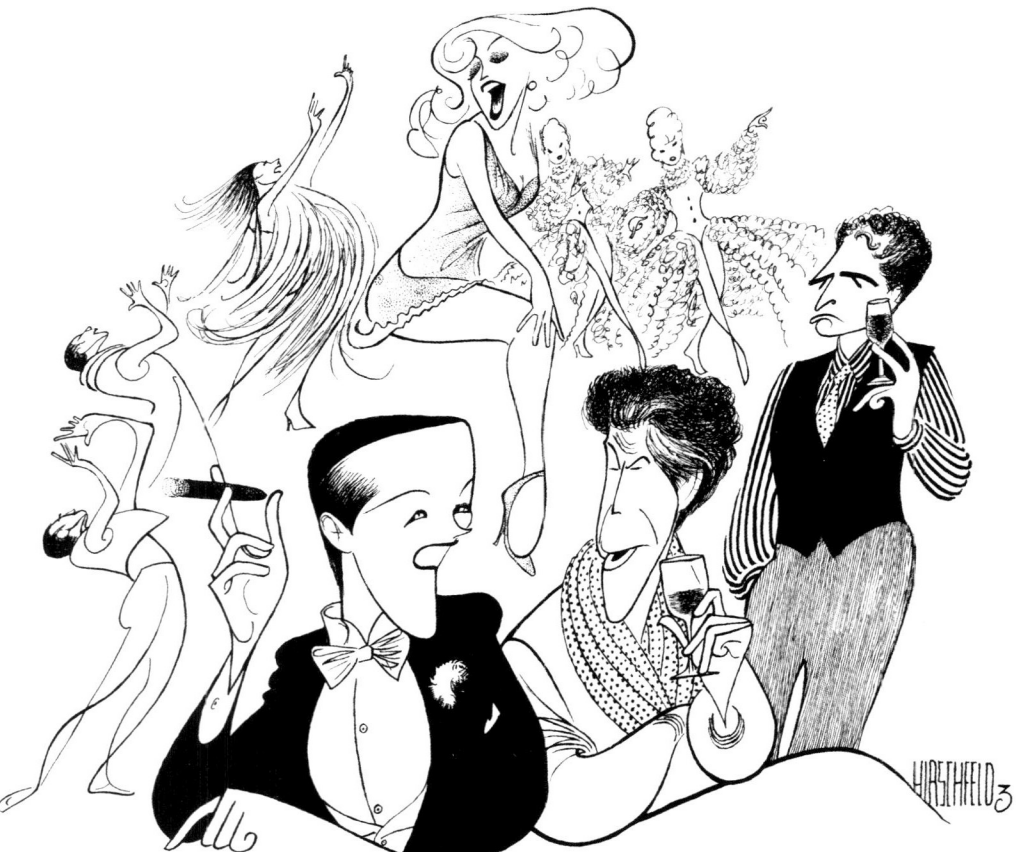

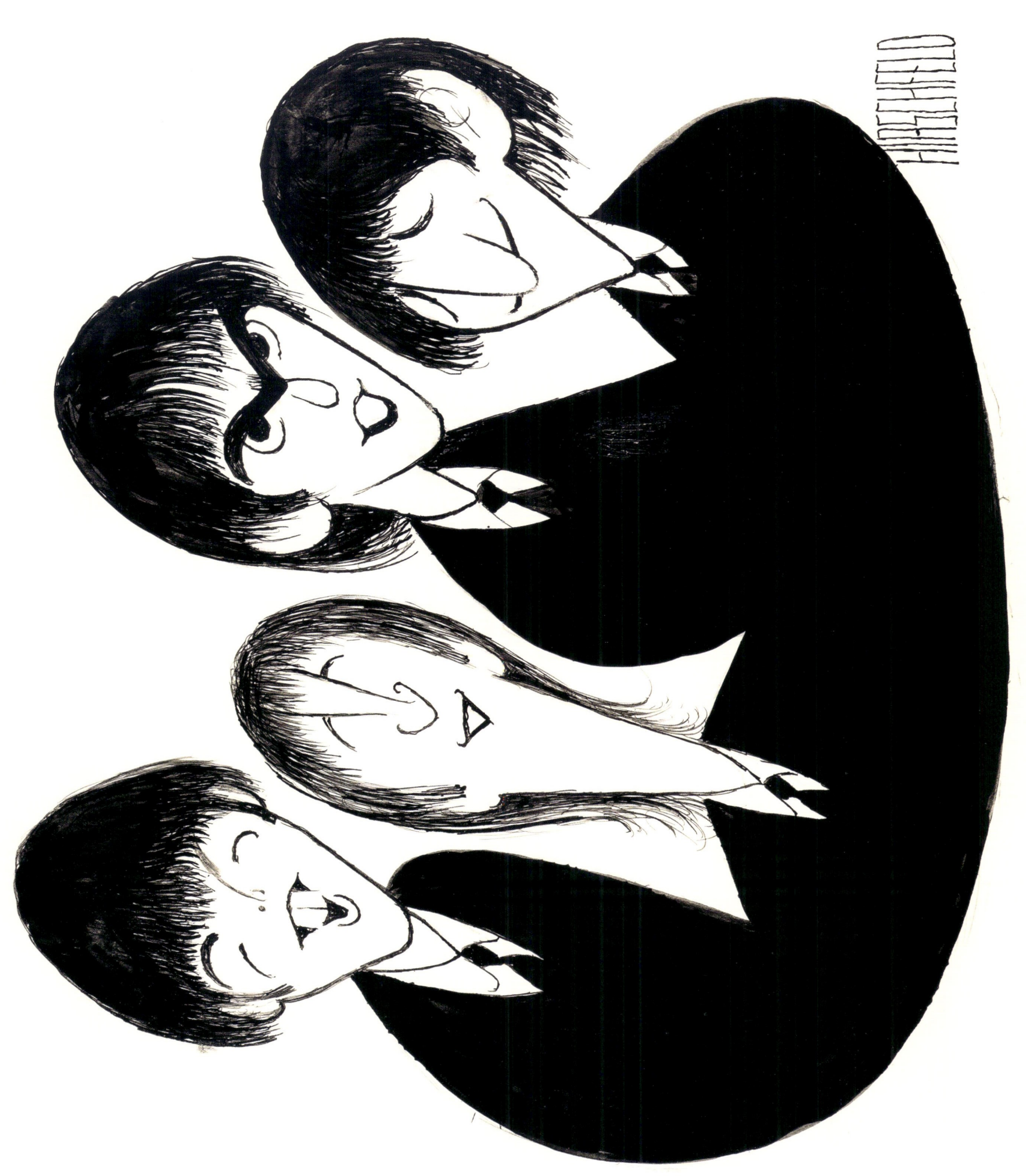

THE BEATLES

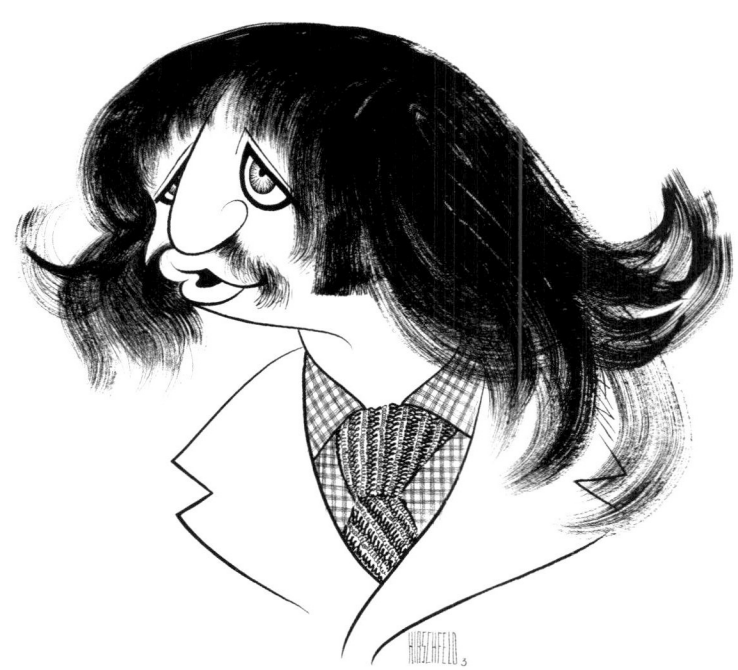

Paul McCartney: b. June 18, 1942
John Lennon: October 9, 1940–December 8, 1980
George Harrison: February 25, 1943–November 29, 2001
Ringo Starr: b. July 7, 1940

Ink on board, 1995

The New York Times, November 12, 1995

"For me," producer Rick Rubin said, "the Beatles are proof of the existence of God." Over the course of an iconic career that lasted just short of a decade, the Beatles achieved unprecedented global influence and commercial success. They fundamentally altered the trajectory of popular music through artistic reinvention and studio experimentation, and redefined singles and record albums as we have now come to know them; they proved that albums could be more commercial than singles, which was a huge paradigm shift in popular music. The Beatles are the best-selling music act of all time, and the most successful act in the history of the *Billboard* charts—selling more than six hundred million records worldwide.

In 1964, they arrived in America and revived a nation still reeling from the assassination of President Kennedy, leading a British Invasion that marked the first time in decades that America was not at the forefront of pop culture. The Beatles so dominated American music that any recording before their arrival was soon referred to as an "oldie."

Hirschfeld's first drawing of the Beatles appeared in May 1964 as part of his "Famous Feuds" series, squaring off against the Singing Nun, who at the time was battling the Fab Four for dominance on the pop charts. "They really were just sweet young kids when they arrived," Hirschfeld remembered, "and I was just as enchanted with them as everyone else. I even enjoyed their music."

Although Hirschfeld drew a much-longer-haired John Lennon and Ringo Starr in the 1960s, he didn't draw the band again until 1990 for a private commission which was later published as a limited-edition lithograph. Hirschfeld decided to draw the mop tops as they looked when they first arrived in America: a four-headed creature that changed music—and the world—forever. He drew them again from this period for this drawing, which appeared when *The Beatles Anthology* was released in 1995.

TOP
Ringo Starr, 1969
This portrait appeared at the time Ringo was striking out on his own as an actor in *The Magic Christian*. Hirschfeld liked this drawing enough that he hung it on the stairwell in his studio. It was later published as a limited-edition etching in 1975

RIGHT
"Famous Feuds: The Beatles vs. Sister Sourire, The Singing Nun," 1964
Hirschfeld's "Famous Feuds" was a regular feature in *Show* magazine in 1963 and 1964.

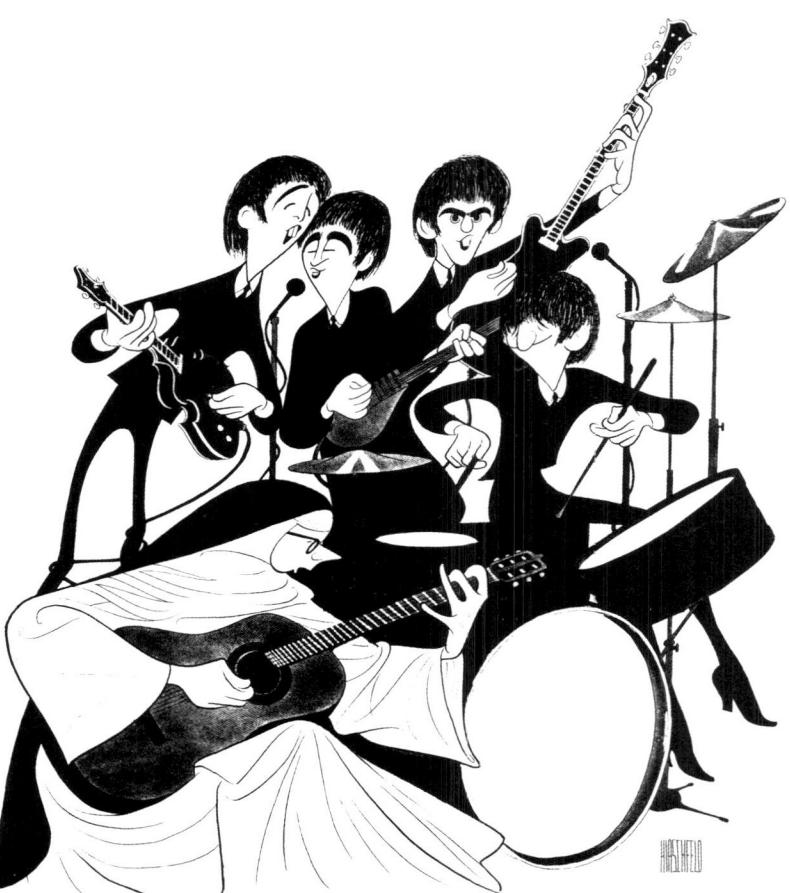

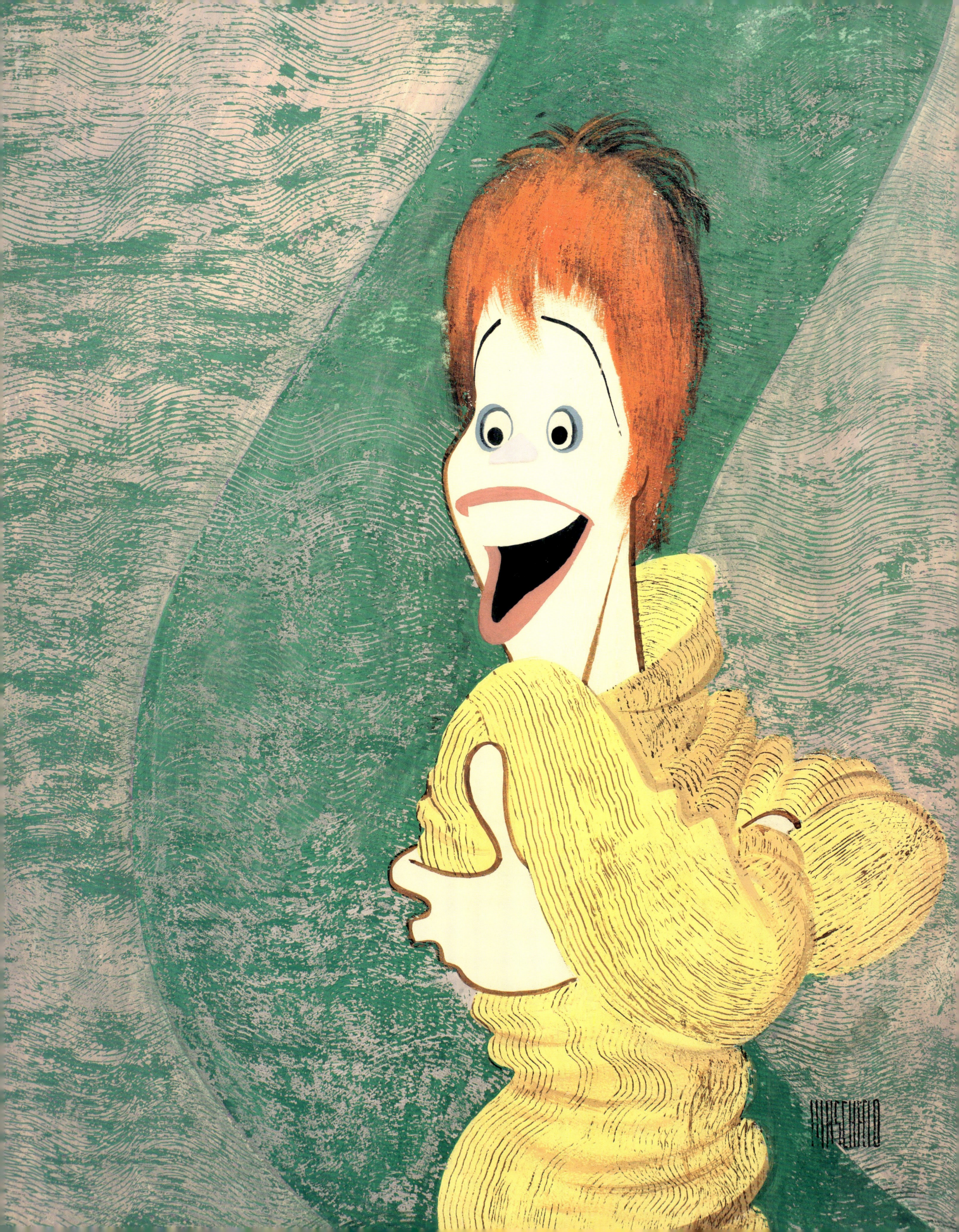

CAROL BURNETT

b. April 26, 1933

Acrylic, gouache, and ink, 1970

TV Guide cover, April 11, 1970

Carol Burnett is a caricature, or at least she played one on television. Over the eleven-year run of her eponymous TV variety show, this beloved icon played several recurring characters that were parodies or exaggerations of different kinds of people. Whether she was playing the Charwoman or "Nora" Desmond from *Sunset Boulevard*, a leading lady on a soap opera or an older sister alongside an inspired ensemble that included Tim Conway, Harvey Korman, and Vicki Lawrence, Burnett made the characters come alive with stylized movements, humorous Bob Mackie–designed costumes, and sharp comic writing. Like Hirschfeld, her caricatures were never meant to be pejorative, but rather they celebrated the unique personality of those she portrayed.

Hirschfeld enjoyed drawing Burnett because, in his eyes, she had "a clown's face, a real comic face." He first saw her in her Tony-nominated breakout role on Broadway in *Once Upon a Mattress* in 1959, and drew the poster for her second Broadway show, *Fade Out – Fade In*, which, despite having a book and lyrics by Betty Comden and Adolph Green, music by Jule Styne, and direction by George Abbott, was a hit only when Burnett was in it.

Hirschfeld painted this unusual portrait for the cover of *TV Guide* when Burnett was at the height of her popularity on

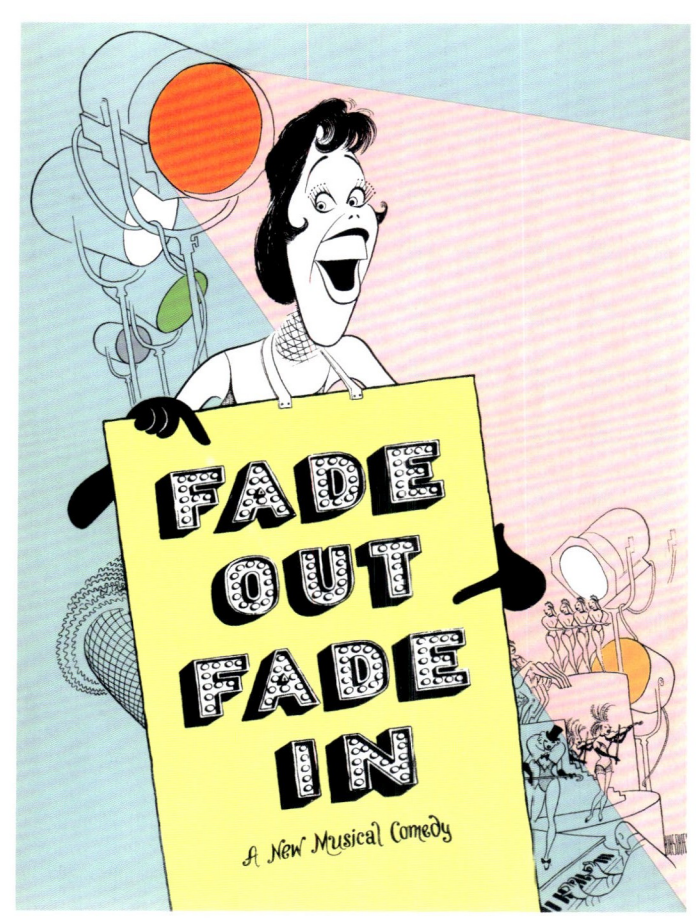

television in *The Carol Burnett Show*, the first time a variety show had been led by a woman. The program ran from 1967 to 1978 and won twenty-five Emmy Awards. When she returned with a new show in 1990 called *Carol Burnett & Company*, Hirschfeld drew her again—the only time he drew a performer twice for the cover of *TV Guide*.

TOP

Fade Out – Fade In, 1964

Poster for a Broadway musical about Hollywood

RIGHT

The Front Page, 1974

LEFT TO RIGHT: Carol Burnett, Jack Lemmon, Walter Matthau, and Billy Wilder on the set of the film adaptation of the Broadway play

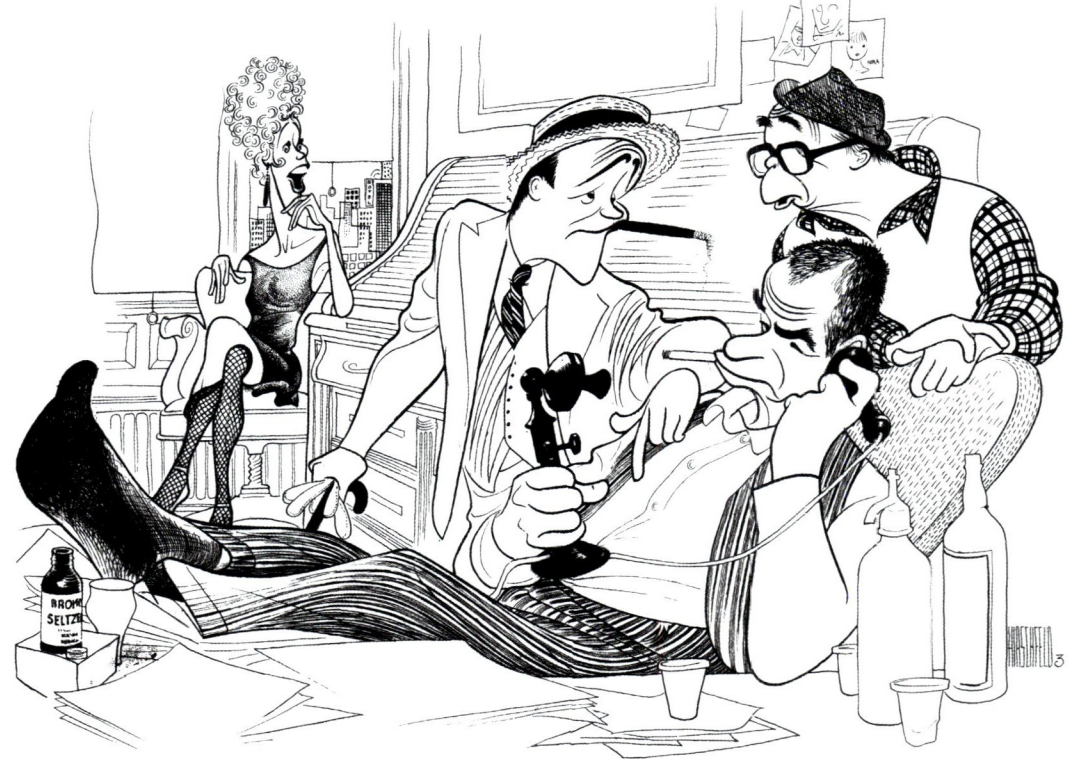

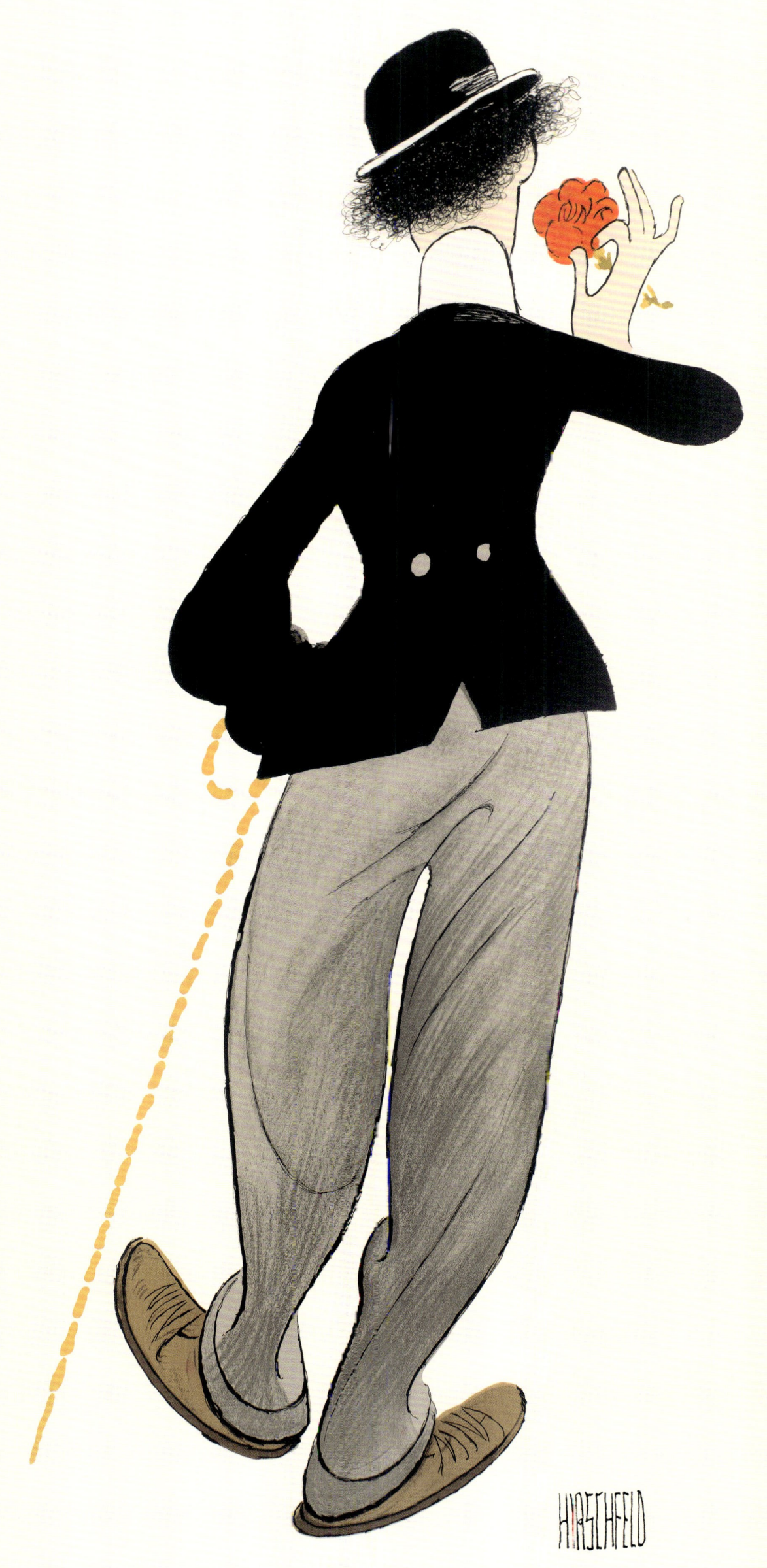

CHARLIE CHAPLIN

April 16, 1889–December 25, 1977

Ink on board, 1941

Promotional campaign for *The Great Dictator*, 1941

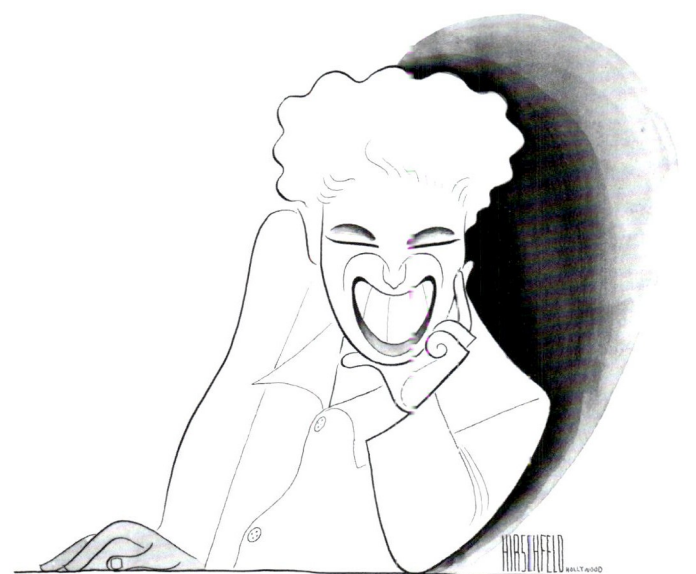

Charlie Chaplin was a comic actor, filmmaker, and composer who rose to fame in the era of silent film, becoming an international icon through his screen persona, the Tramp. His derby hat, loose-fitting pants, large shoes, and tiny mustache became instantly identifiable around the world. Even when movies began to talk, Chaplin resisted and made two more mostly silent films, *City Lights* (1931) and *Modern Times* (1936), that are not only among his greatest works but considered two of the 100 greatest American films of all time by the American Film Institute (AFI), coming in at numbers 76 and 81, respectively.

Hirschfeld first drew the multihyphenate for a poster for the rerelease of his 1919 film short *Sunnyside*, in 1927, the first of thirty-three images. The two men met on the island of Bali in 1932. "He was on a round-the-world cruise, and I had been living and painting there," Hirschfeld wrote ten years later. "The motion picture had not yet made its appearance in Bali. On discovering his anonymity, he decided to carry out an experiment. It was then I realized that the mustache, baggy pants, and oversized shoes were of no more importance to Chaplin than the type of quill used by Shakespeare or the frame on any great painting."

For a small audience of island residents, "He proceeded to put [his] pith helmet on his head, and it sprang crazily into the air with a will of its own. Undaunted and with a wonderful look of nonchalance, he tried it again. And again the hat flew off his head. The [locals] howled with laughter . . . That was the experiment. He had wanted to see if the Balinese would laugh at his pantomime. And they did. Chaplin's science is humor and his laboratory the world."

When they met a decade later for Hirschfeld to interview him for *The New York Times*, Hirschfeld wrote, "We talked of many things. He was in great form. I don't remember what he said. He was dancing, laughing, and being the greatest pantomimist I had even seen. White hair, honest blue eyes, a laugh more eloquent than any prose. Young in a way that few youths have even been. Old with a rare dignity. I watched this man who dares to be simple, as fascinated and amused as the first time I saw him in the movies. He talks and thinks pictorially, knowing every second how he looks and not caring what he says."

Hirschfeld concluded, "He trusts his instincts rather than his intellect. If a thing seems right or feels right, he accepts it. His art is not cerebral, it's natural. Chaplin looks right because he is . . . [He] has exploited to the full his endowed talents. He trusts and never underrates his genius. He will sometimes do nothing for months, waiting for the custard pie of creation to smack him. He is a man with both feet firmly planted in the clouds."

Hirschfeld captured Chaplin walking away, a pose at the end of many of the comedian's films, most famously in *The Circus* (1928), but later with Paulette Goddard in *Modern Times*. The image is so iconic that Hirschfeld returned to it several times, including as his final image of Chaplin in late 2002.

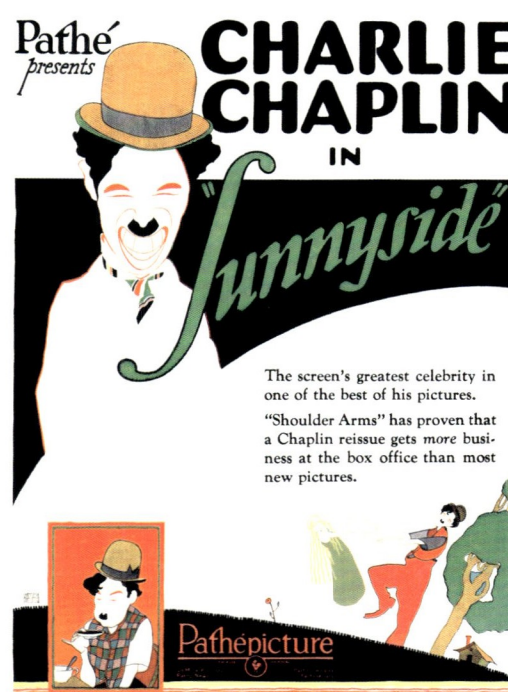

ABOVE

Charlie Chaplin, 1942

Hirschfeld drew this image of Chaplin out of costume for his profile of the comedian in *The New York Times*.

LEFT

Sunnyside, 1927

Hirschfeld's first drawing of Chaplin appeared in a Pathé studio "yearbook," a publication given to theater owners as a catalogue of the studio's releases for the coming year.

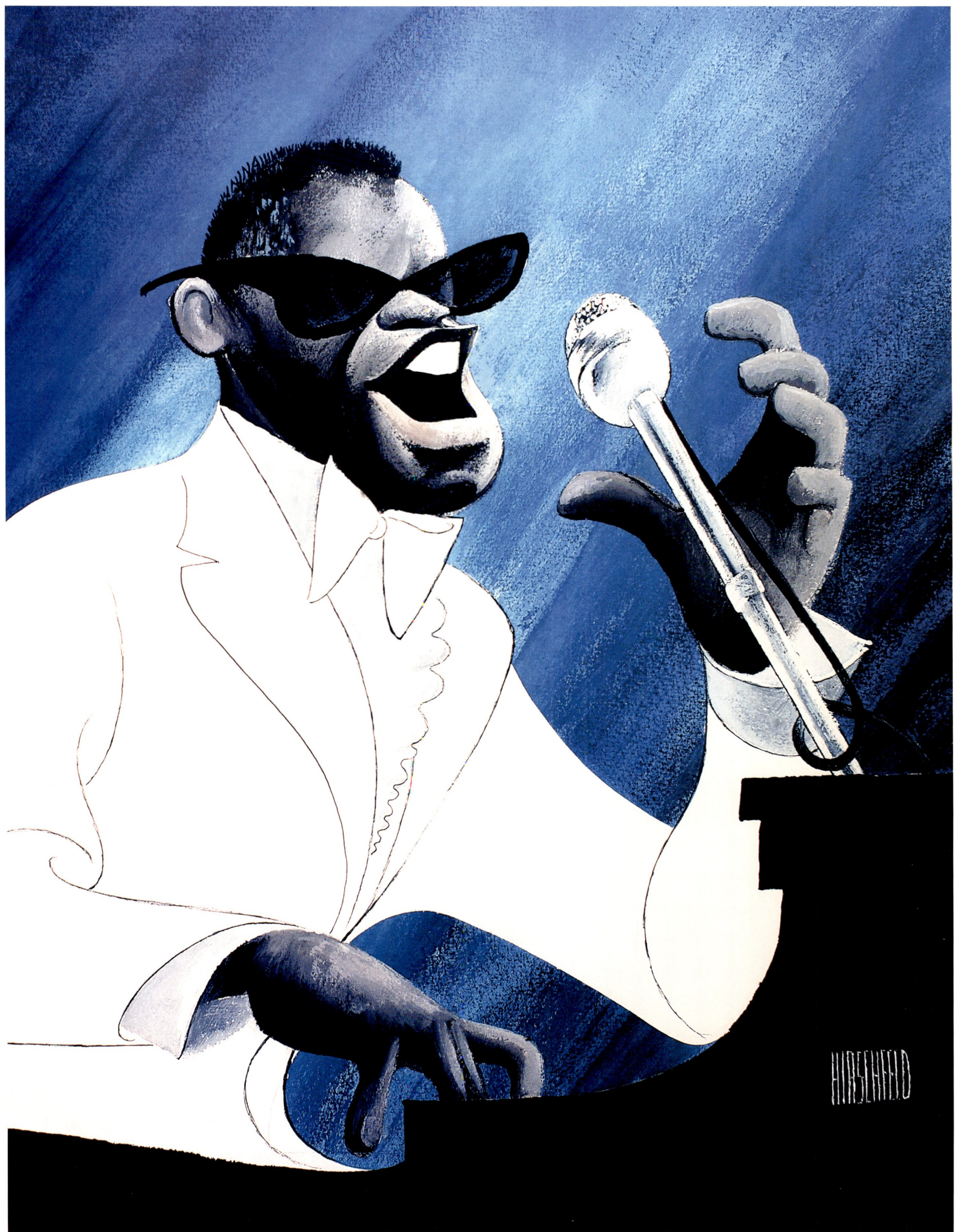

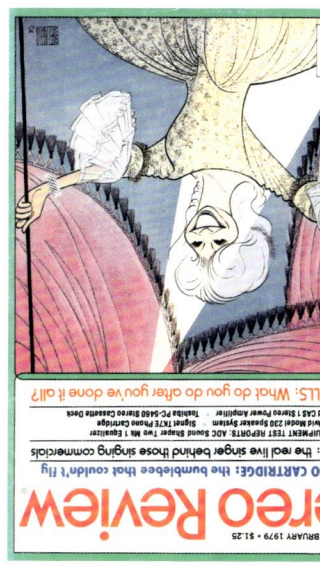

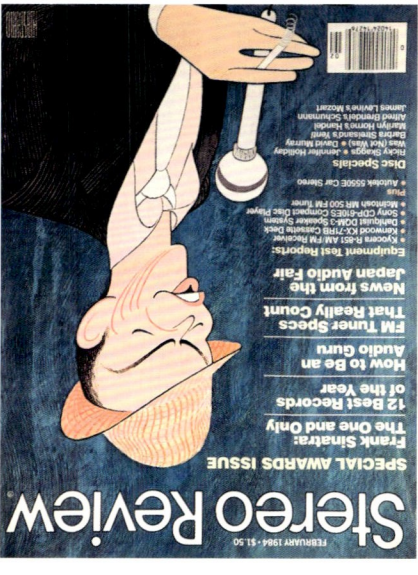

RAY CHARLES

September 23, 1930–June 10, 2004
Gouache on board, 1985
Stereo Review cover, February 1986

Frank Sinatra simply called him "genius." Most of his friends called him "Brother Ray," Billy Joel said, "This may sound like sacrilege, but I think Ray Charles was more important than Elvis Presley."

As a singer, songwriter, and keyboardist, Ray Charles is regarded as one of the most iconic and influential musicians in history. He won seventeen Grammy Awards and a Grammy Lifetime Achievement Award, and ten of his recordings have been inducted into the Grammy Hall of Fame. In 1986, he was one of the inaugural inductees at the Rock & Roll Hall of Fame.

Charles started making national chart-topping records in 1954 with the hits "I Got a Woman" and "What'd I Say" before making history with songs like "Hit the Road Jack" and "Georgia on My Mind." When this artwork first appeared in *Stereo Review* magazine in 1986, Charles had just participated in the musical supergroup recording of "We Are the World."

Stereo Review played a key role in making hi-fi a popular and accessible hobby. From its inception as *HiFi & Music Review* in 1958, the magazine has been an essential part of audiophiles' lives. Hirschfeld had been a contributor since 1959, and from 1977 to 1988 the magazine turned to him annually for striking full-color portraits of music's most important figures, including Isaac Stern, Irving Berlin, and Sinatra. "Look, let's face it," Charles once said. "Good music is good music. I don't care if it's Beethoven, Chopin, blues, rock. Music's been around a long time, and there's going to be music long after Ray Charles is dead. I just want to make my mark, leave something musically good behind. If it's a big record, that's the frosting on the cake. But the music's the main deal."

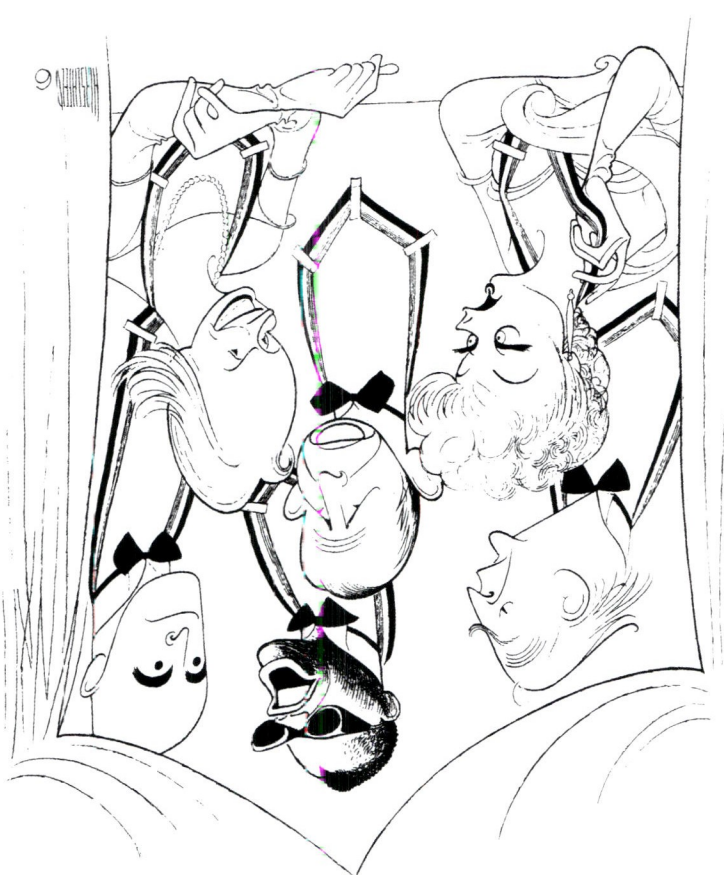

ABOVE
Kennedy Center Honors, 1986
LEFT TO RIGHT: Yehudi Menuhin, Lucille Ball, Hume Cronyn, Ray Charles, Jessica Tandy, and Antony Tudor

BELOW
Frank Sinatra, 1984; Beverly Sills, 1979; and Earl Hines, 1980
Covers and poster for Stereo Review

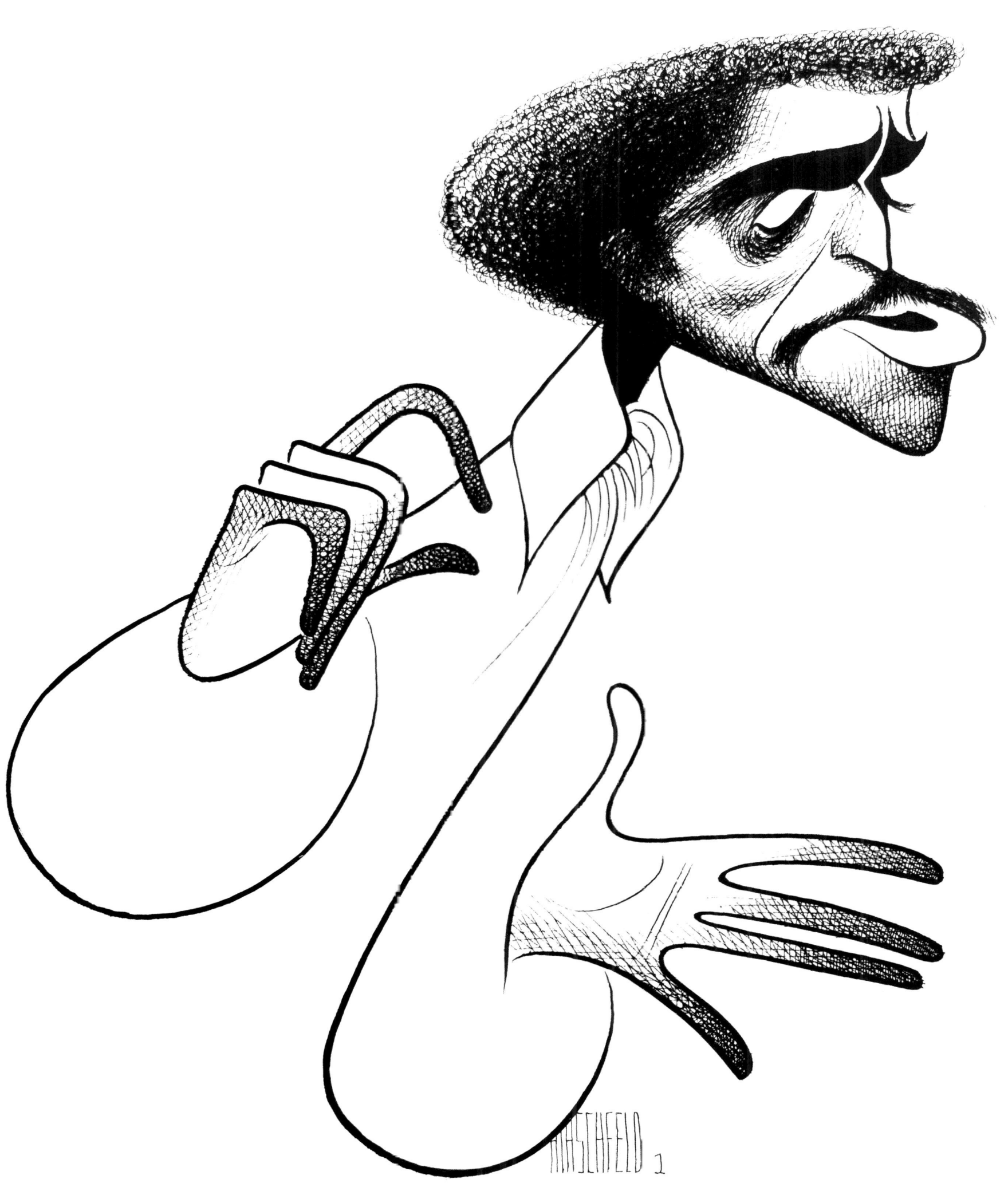

SAMMY DAVIS JR.

December 8, 1925–May 16, 1990

Ink on board, 1974

The New York Times, April 21, 1974

"Sammy Davis Jr. has always been a powerhouse of a performer. He can tapdance with thunder, mimic his peers, and sing Frank Sinatra songs as well as Frank Sinatra. He is a natural choice for a one-man show," *The New York Times* wrote four days after Hirschfeld's drawing of the icon appeared in the same paper. "Give Mr. Davis a spotlight and with his energy and personality he could easily entertain us for hours. He could simply offer a selection of his best material or perhaps he could guide us through his work while talking about his life, from his early days in vaudeville . . . and on to today."

Over forty-six years, Hirschfeld drew Davis twenty-eight times, beginning in 1955 when he was still performing in nightclubs with his father in the Will Mastin Trio. Soon there were drawings of Davis's film roles, including those in *Anna Lucasta* and *Porgy and Bess* (he played Sportin' Life). Davis's membership in the Rat Pack alongside Sinatra and Dean Martin can also be seen in drawings from the 1960s.

Davis captivated Broadway with his performance in the musical adaptation of Clifford Odets's *Golden Boy*. The role was transposed as a young man from Harlem who turns to prizefighting as a means to better himself. His love interest was Paula Wayne, who was white, and theirs was the first interracial kiss in Broadway's history.

Davis Jr.'s popularity helped break the race barrier of the segregated entertainment industry. He converted to Judaism in 1960 after recuperating from a car accident in which he lost an eye. Davis felt there were many similarities between the oppression of Jewish and Black people. One day, on a golf course with Jack Benny, Benny asked what his handicap was. "Handicap?" Davis replied. "Talk about handicap. I'm a one-eyed Negro who's Jewish."

TOP

Golden Boy, 1964

Sammy Davis Jr. and Paula Wayne

RIGHT

Evening at Pops, 1989

John Williams, Carol Channing, and Sammy Davis Jr.

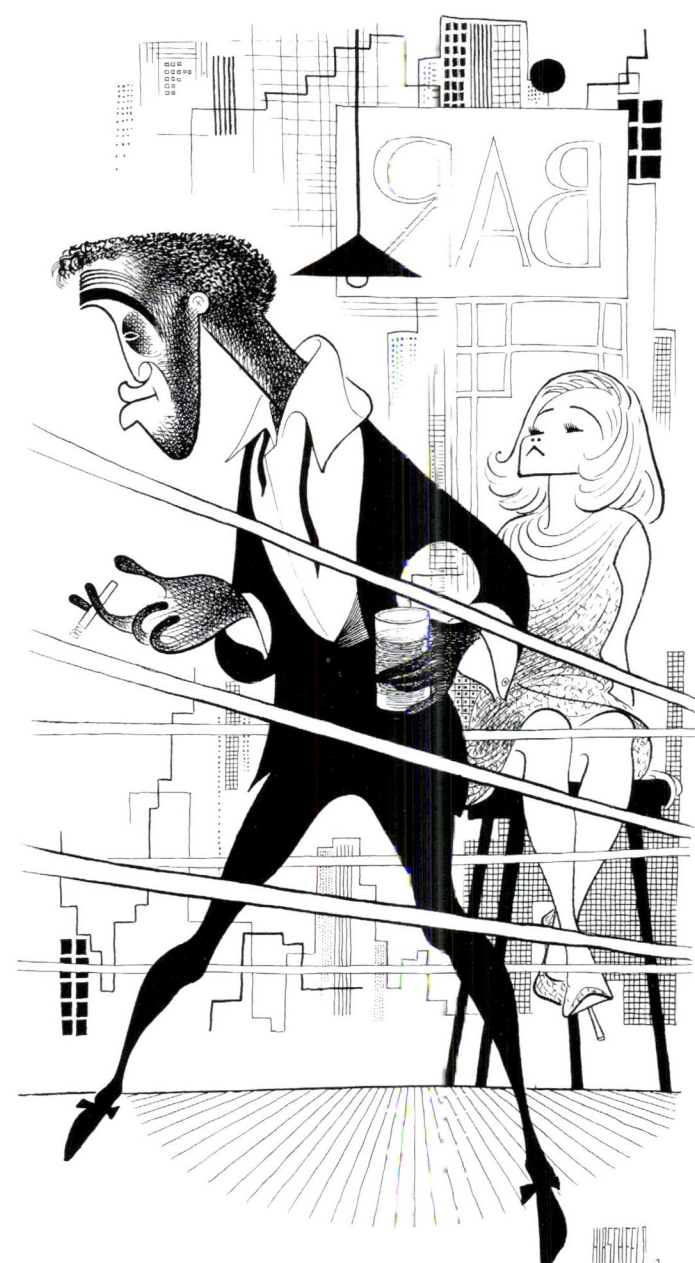

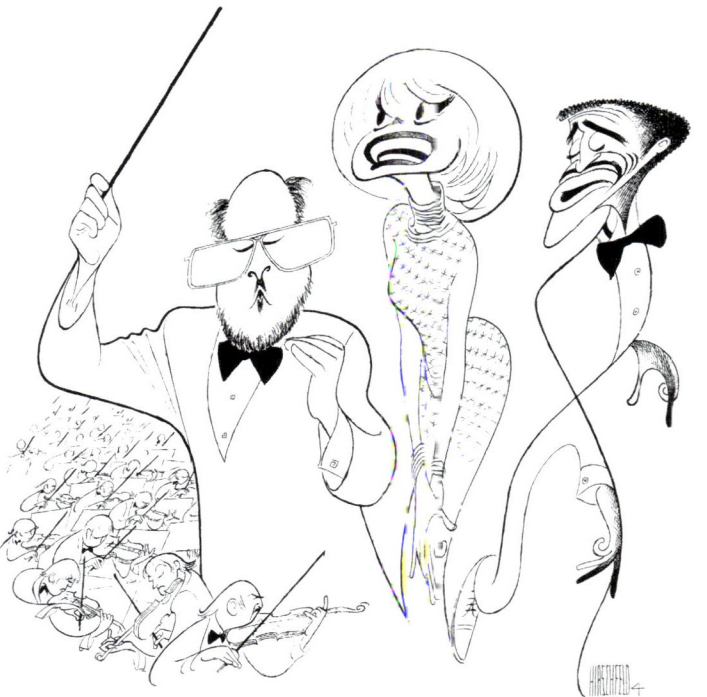

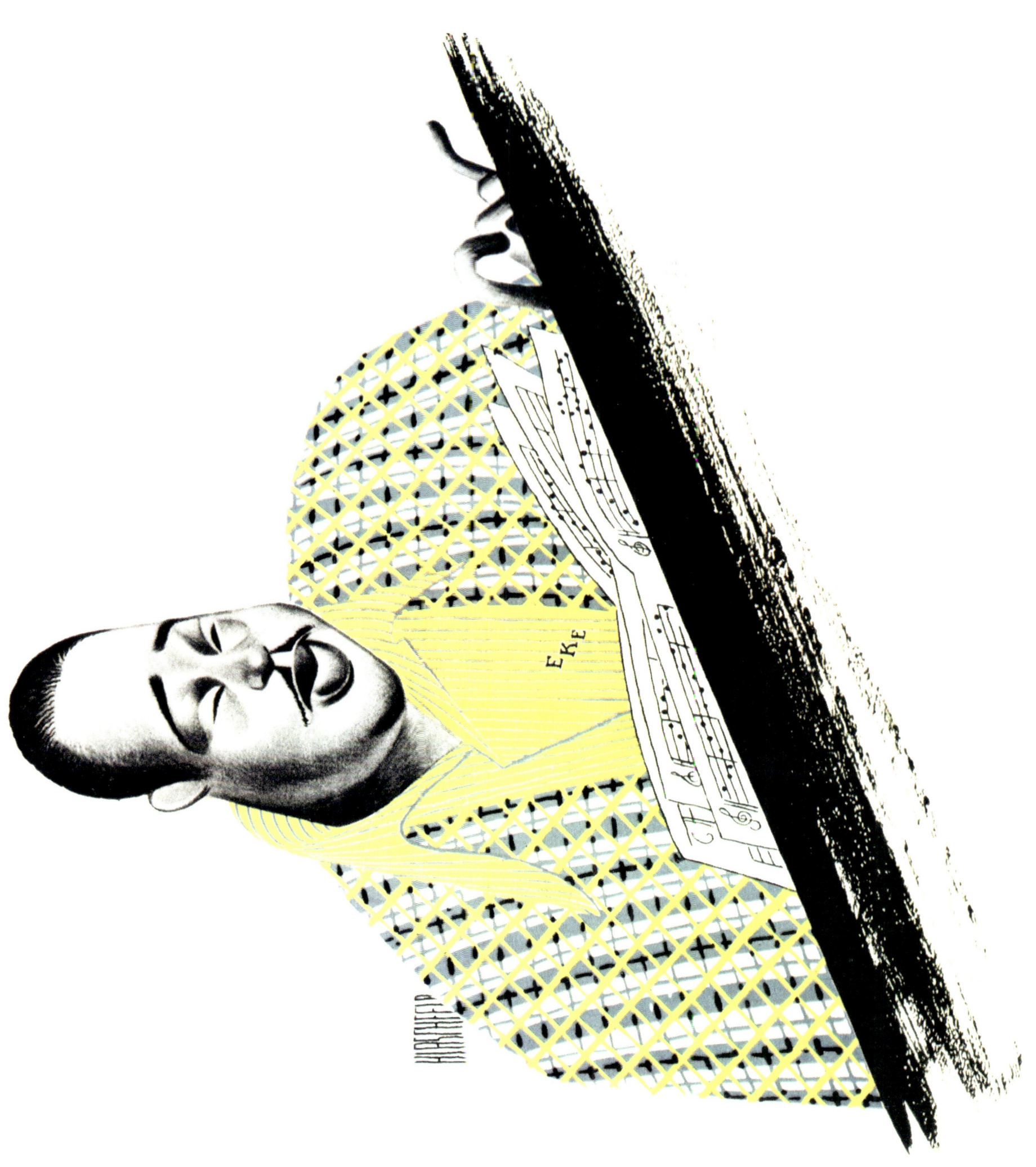

DUKE ELLINGTON

April 29, 1899–May 24, 1974

Ink and gouache on board, 1946

Seventeen, January 1946

Hirschfeld's drawings have a rhythm and harmony that can make them sing to the viewer. He enjoyed music of all kinds, but he loved "hot jazz" and had more records by Duke Ellington and Louis Armstrong than any other musicians in his collection of 78s, the medium of his youth. Hirschfeld frequently went to concerts in night-clubs, concert halls, and barrooms, and was a regular at rehearsals and after-hours jam sessions, too.

In 1931, Hirschfeld helped Ellington deal with racism on his first national tour. Ellington's manager, Irving Mills, understood that racism would make many editors and theater owners avoid publishing a photo of a Black man. So Mills hired Hirschfeld to produce a compelling portrait of the serious musician and composer.

In Hirschfeld's drawings, often the color of a man's skin was of no more impor-tance than the color of his costume. Hirschfeld's genius was to capture the essence of his subject's character and distill the image in pure line. The iconic portrait of Elling-ton featured here was so effective that it was used to promote his tours for at least three years.

By 1946, Ellington proved to be popular as a composer, pianist, arranger, band-leader, and personality, prompting *Seventeen* to include him in a two-year series of profiles on the jazz titans of the day—all with color portraits by Hirschfeld.

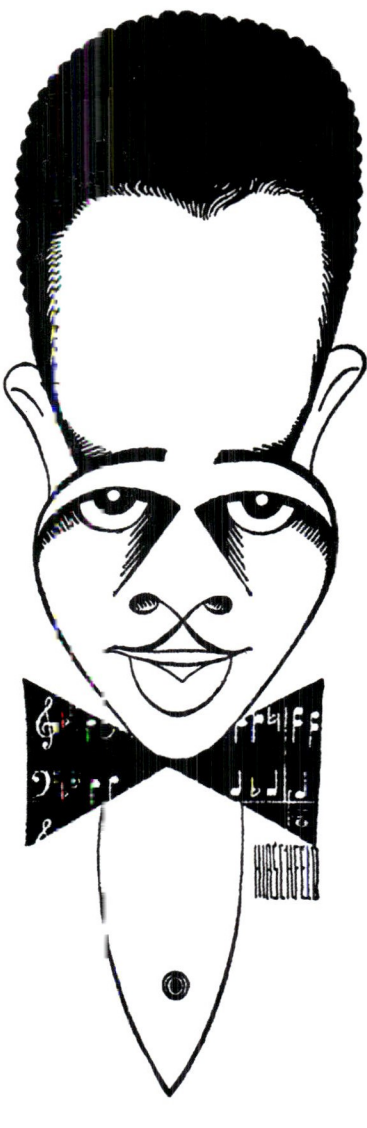

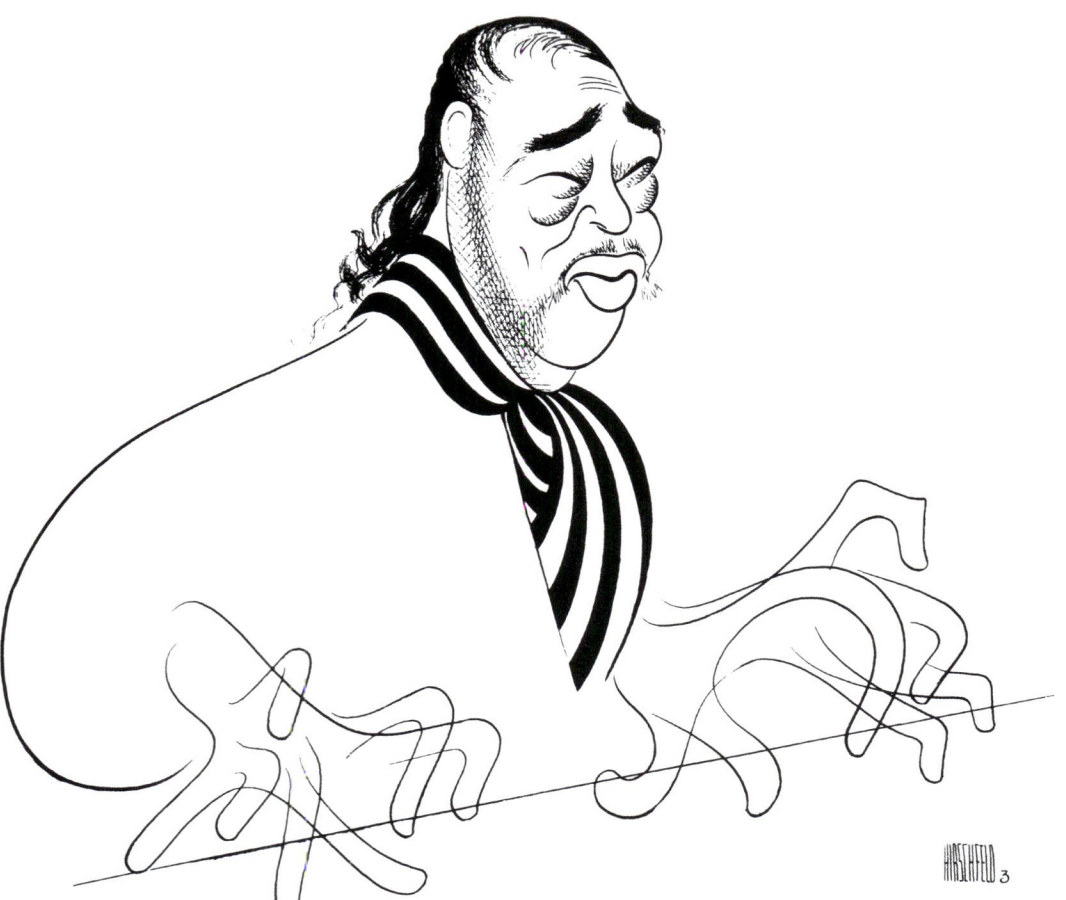

ABOVE

Duke Ellington, 1931

Ellington scholar Steven Lasker wrote that this portrait "debuted in print on April 19, 1931, in *The Des Moines Register*, above a caption that read 'Duke Ellington, Harlem king of jazz,' featured with his orchestra on Paramount vaudeville bill.'" Lasker also noted it "was one of the most frequently used designs in theatre ads for Ellington during the early and mid-1930s." In 1992, the Smithsonian asked Hirschfeld to re-create his 1931 drawing. This work was later published as a limited-edition lithograph.

LEFT

Duke Ellington, 1973

The television special *Duke Ellington . . . We Love You Madly*, an all-star tribute from February 11, 1973, was heralded in *The New York Times* with this drawing. It was later published as a limited-edition etching in 1991.

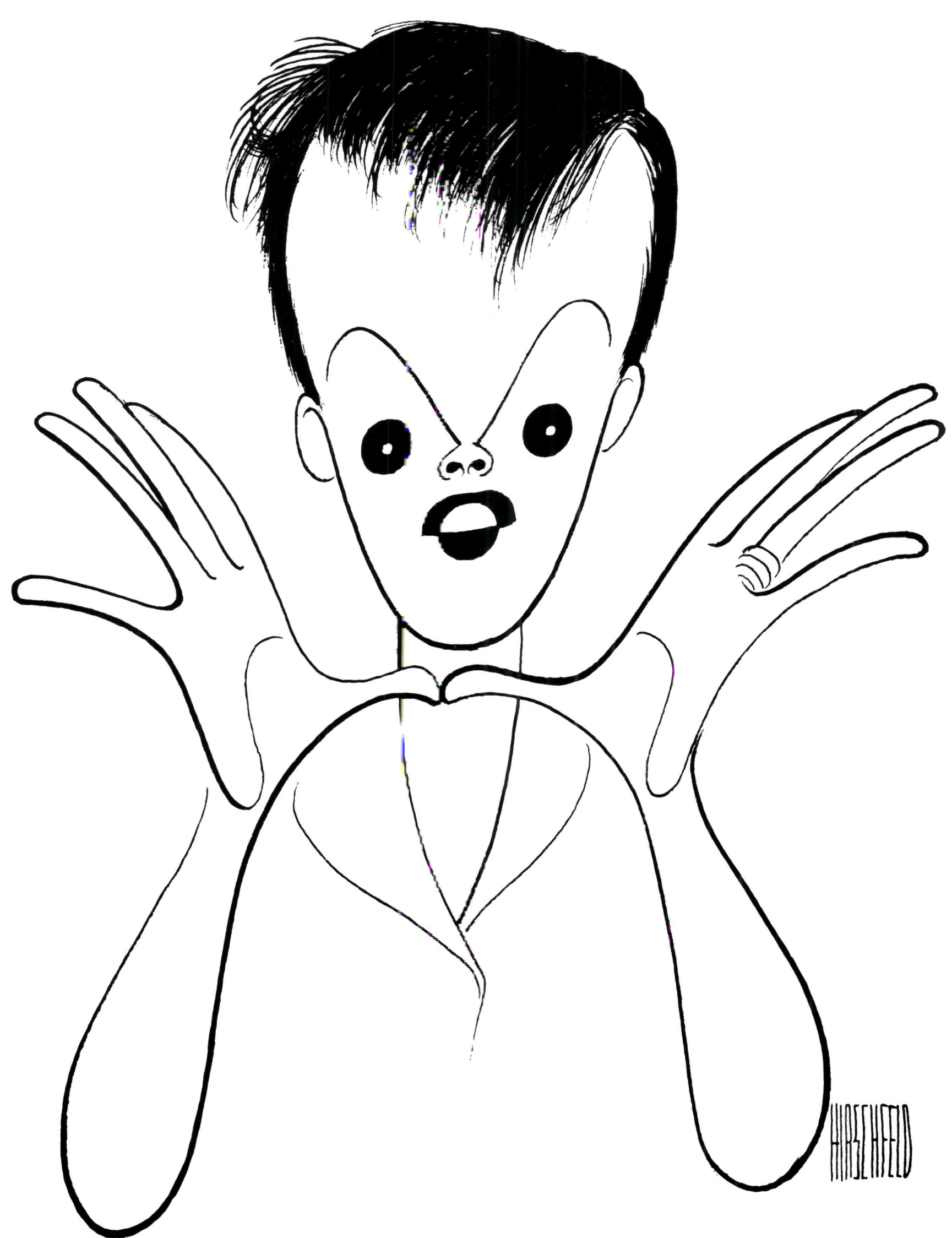

JUDY GARLAND

June 10, 1922–June 22, 1969

Ink on board, 1977

Advertisement for *A Star Is Born* on IBM's
Movies to Remember TV series, 1977

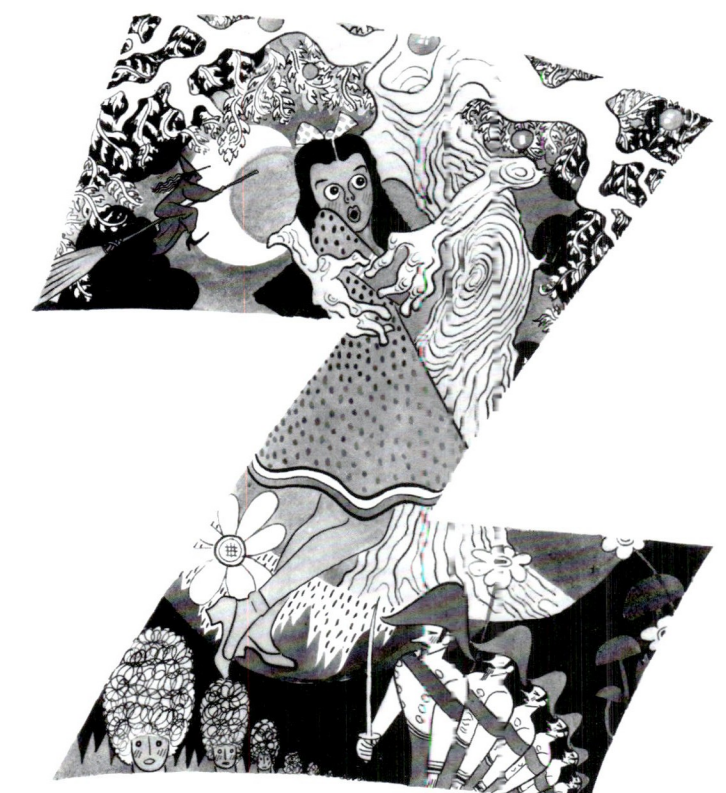

Judy Garland, considered one of the greatest American entertainers of the twentieth century, was a triple threat, due to her ability to sing, act, and dance equally well. Writer Doug Strassler said Garland was "more than an icon. Like Charlie Chaplin and Lucille Ball, she created a template that the powers that be have forever been trying, with varied levels of success, to replicate."

Garland became a star when she was seventeen years old, playing Dorothy Gale in the 1939 MGM film *The Wizard of Oz*. Hirschfeld drew almost all the posters for the film's original release. He also contributed promotional drawings and posters for Garland's films in the 1940s, from *Strike Up the Band* (1940) to *Easter Parade* (1948). Garland was one of the studio's top stars, and worked constantly—until the end of the decade, when the drugs and alcohol that helped her deal with studio demands and the pressures of fame started to interfere with her work.

The performer triumphantly returned to the silver screen in 1954 with *A Star Is Born*, alongside James Mason, which she also co-produced. She was in great form, but her bad habits made the filming take much longer than scheduled. While the film was not a commercial success initially, her best song in the film—a torch ballad, "The Man That Got Away"—joined "Over the Rainbow" as a Garland trademark.

Despite her achievements, the public defined Garland by her private life, and her sometimes erratic appearances in later years, ranging from revelatory to ridiculous, helped cement that reputation. Hirschfeld captured these performances as well, including her legendary shows at New York City's Palace Theatre in 1955 and her run of seven shows at the Metropolitan Opera House in 1959.

Garland's live performances toward the end of her career are still remembered by fans who attended them as "peak moments in twentieth-century music," according to Camille Paglia. Garland's obituary in *The New York Times* stated that Garland possessed "a seemingly unquenchable need for her audiences to respond with acclaim and affection. And often, they did, screaming, 'We love you, Judy—we love you.'"

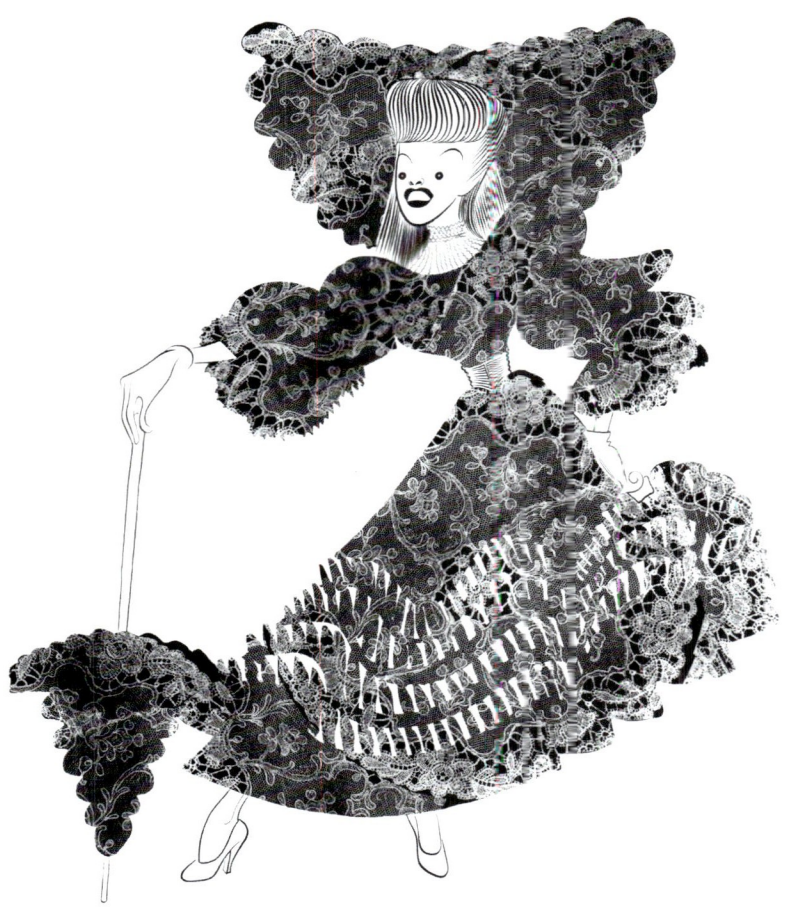

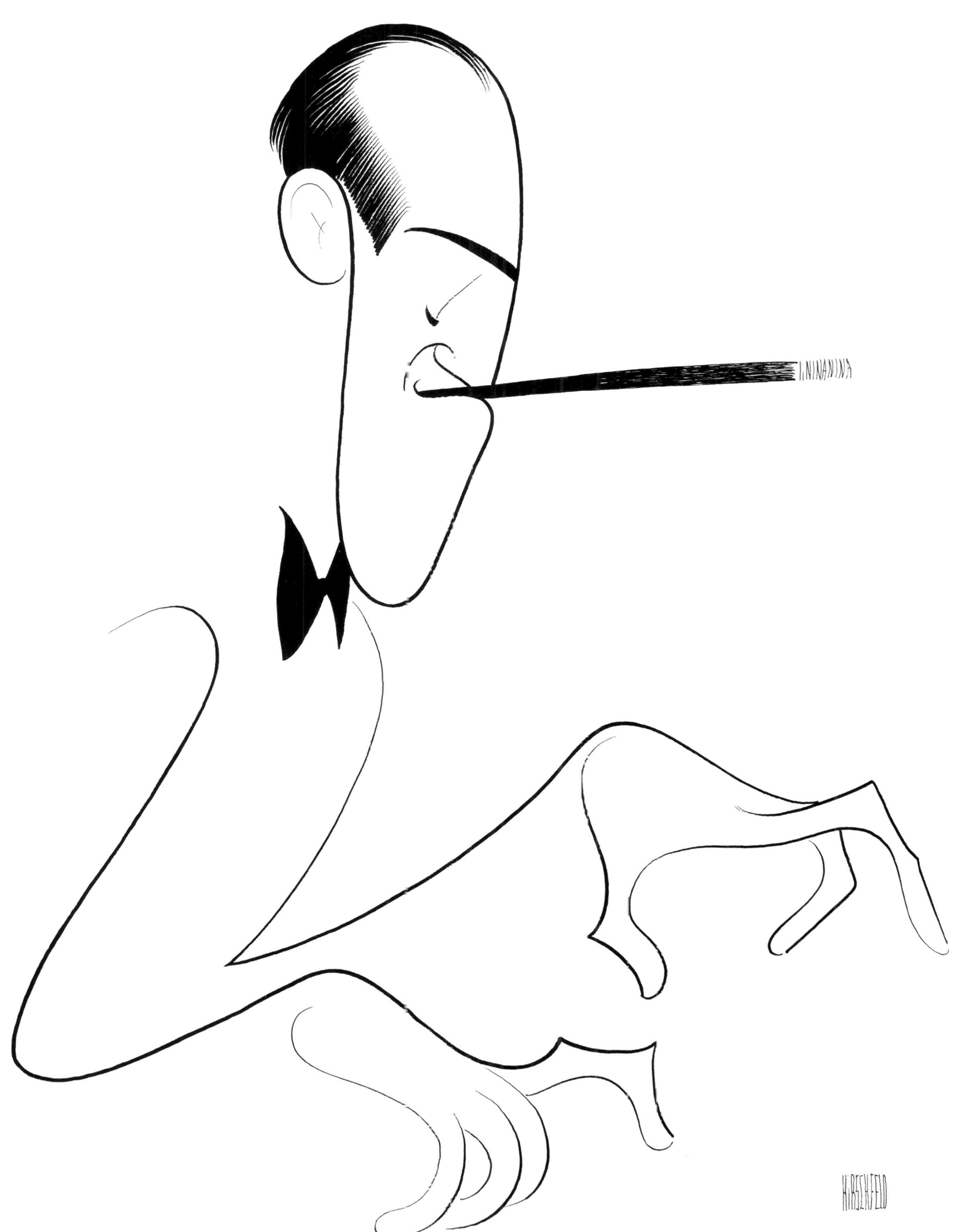

GEORGE GERSHWIN

September 26, 1898–July 11, 1937

Ink on board, c. 1960s

First publication unknown

George Gershwin was an American composer whose works successfully spanned popular music, jazz, and classical. He wrote for Broadway, Hollywood, and the concert stage, collaborating with his brother Ira as lyricist. Their songs have become the bedrock of the Great American Songbook and continue to be performed and recorded for new audiences.

Hirschfeld first met the Gershwins when they were teenagers in Washington Heights. One night in the mid-1920s, while having dinner at the Gershwin family home, Hirschfeld told George of a young pianist who could really play his music—Oscar Levant. So they went to see him perform later that evening at Dave's Blue Room, a joint in the Theater District that had Hirschfeld drawings on the wall, much like the caricatures at Sardi's and the Paris nightclubs that started the trend. The two hit it off, and Levant went on to become well known for his recordings of Gershwin compositions as well as his own music.

Hirschfeld drew George against a collaged fragment of his score for the Broadway musical *Strike Up the Band* (1930) in his first published drawing of the composer. Just as Hirschfeld and his contemporaries introduced aspects of modern art into their work, Gershwin introduced elements of modern music at the top of this show in his overture, which has since become a standalone concert work.

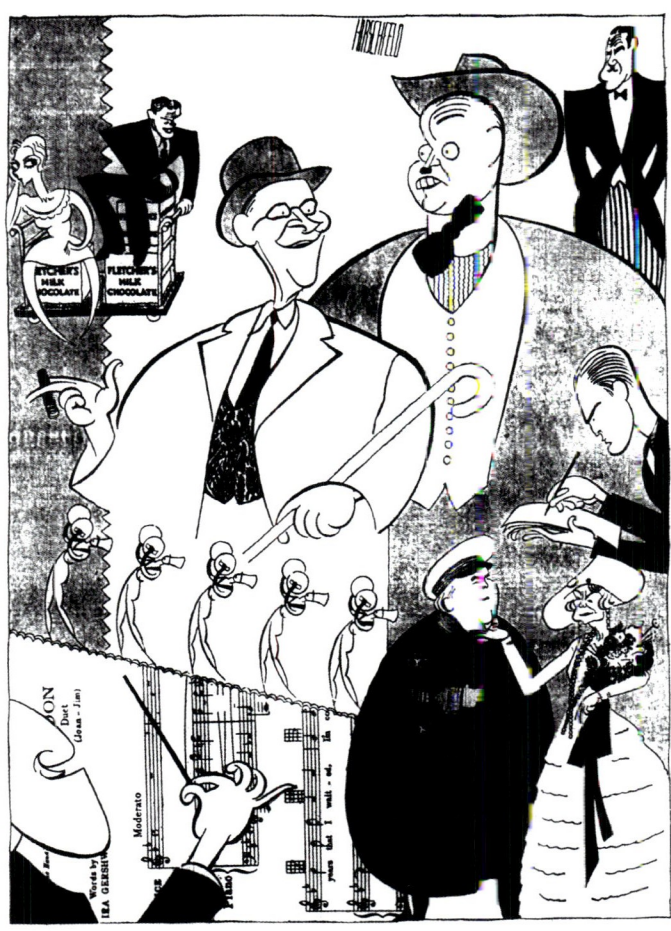

Hirschfeld also created illustrations for the Gershwin "folk opera," *Porgy and Bess*, in 1935, when it premiered on Broadway. Hirschfeld's first of more than 250 album covers was for a selection of songs from the opera.

A portrait of the brothers for a 1953 album cover, *Gershwin Rarities: Volume 1*, became the iconic visual representation of the team for five decades, used countless times for concerts, performances, and tributes. Hirschfeld and the Gershwins were so synonymous that when the Gershwin estate planned for the songwriting team's centennial in 1997, they turned to Hirschfeld for their logo.

For younger audiences, their introduction to the worlds of Gershwin and Hirschfeld came in Disney's *Fantasia 2000*. Eric and Susan Goldberg animated Hirschfeld drawings, including a portrait of Gershwin, for a day in the life of Manhattan c. 1935, scored to Gershwin's "Rhapsody in Blue," arguably the most popular part of the film.

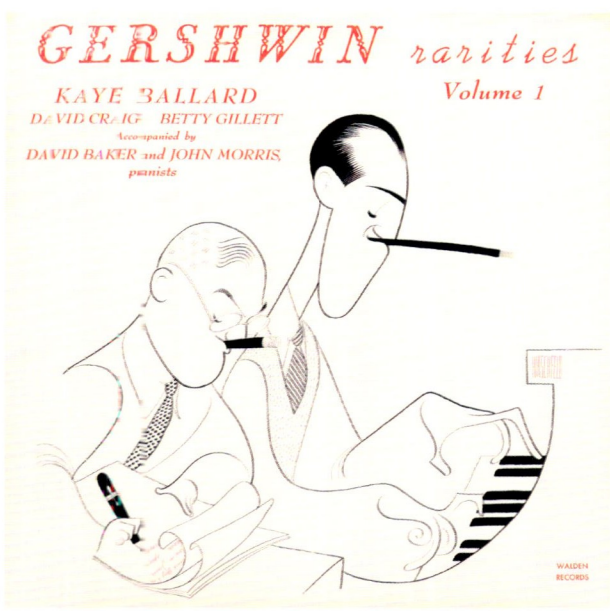

ABOVE

Strike Up the Band, 1930

LEFT TO RIGHT: George Gershwin, Doris Carson, Gordon Smith, Bobby Clark, Paul McCullough, Dudley Clements, Blanche Ring, and Robert Benchley

LEFT

George and Ira Gershwin, 1953

Gershwin Rarities Volume 1, Walden Records

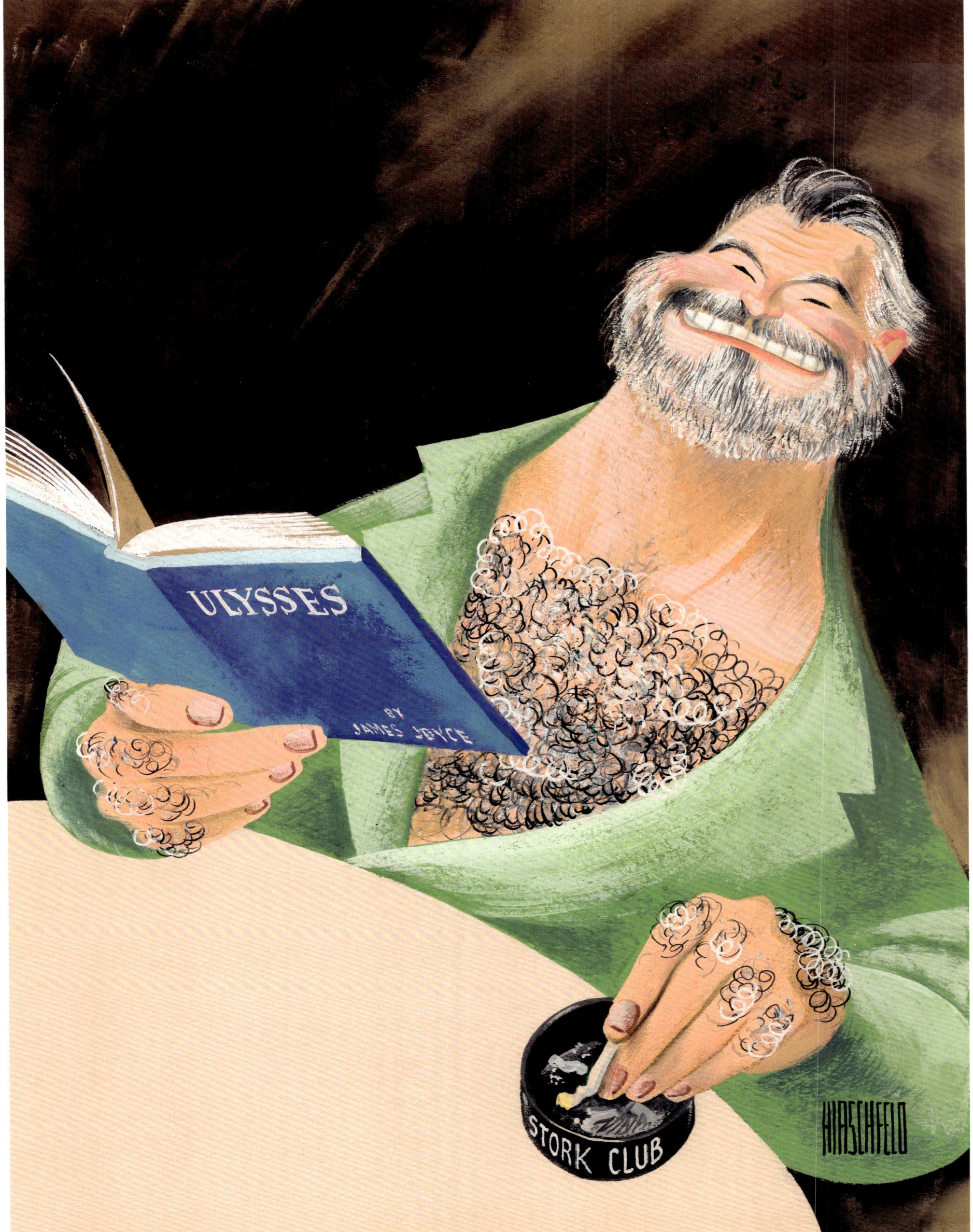

ERNEST HEMINGWAY

July 21, 1899–July 2, 1961

Gouache on board, 1950

Cover for *American Mercury*, November 1950

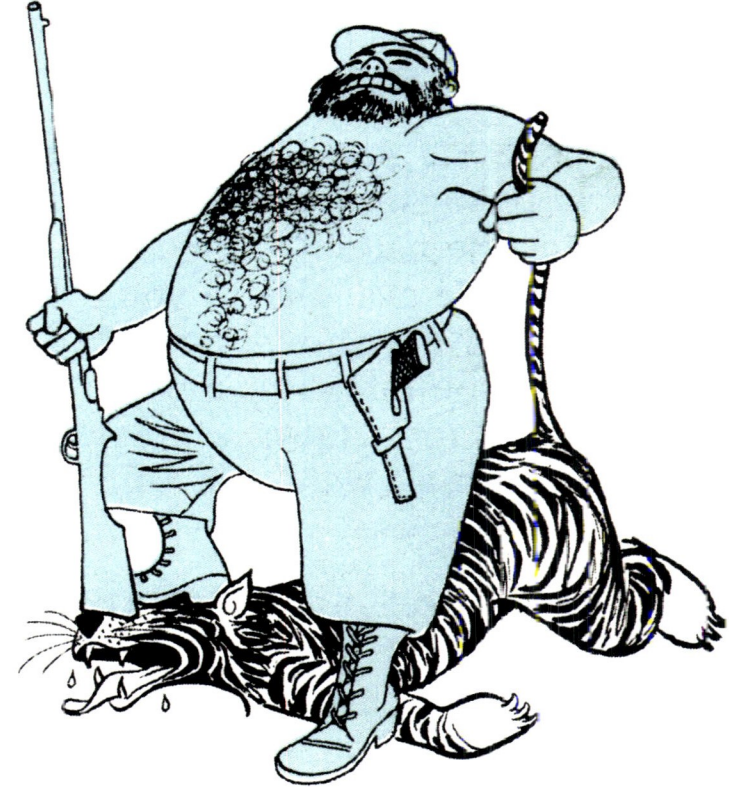

Ernest Hemingway was an iconic novelist, short story writer, and journalist. His crisp, clear style became a template for generations of writers, and several of his works are considered classics of American literature, including *The Sun Also Rises* and *A Farewell to Arms*. In 1953, Hemingway was awarded the Pulitzer Prize for Fiction and received the Nobel Prize in Literature in 1954. The public feasted on reports of Hemingway's risk-taking lifestyle, and his outspoken, often blunt opinions were treated as news.

Hirschfeld met Hemingway in Paris in 1925, before the writer had published any of his acclaimed novels. Although the artist felt Hemingway was a bit of a bully, he nevertheless purchased a copy of Hemingway's first book, *Three Stories and Ten Poems*, which remained in Hirschfeld's library for the rest of his life. Hirschfeld also provided illustrations for the film adaptations of Hemingway's works, including *For Whom the Bell Tolls* (1943), starring Gary Cooper and Ingrid Bergman, and *The Old Man and the Sea* (1958), starring Spencer Tracy.

Many of Hirschfeld's closest friends were writers, including a long association and collaboration with humorist S. J. Perelman. But the writers he is most associated with are those of the Algonquin Round Table, an elite group that included publishers and critics in New York City who met frequently for lunch at the Algonquin Hotel in the 1920s, including Dorothy Parker, George S. Kaufman, and Robert Benchley. Hirschfeld had professional and personal connections with all of the Round Table members, and in 1962 was asked to draw the group for *Horizon* magazine. That image has become the de facto logo of the famed group, and was even included in the Algonquin Round Table entry of the *Encyclopedia Brittanica*.

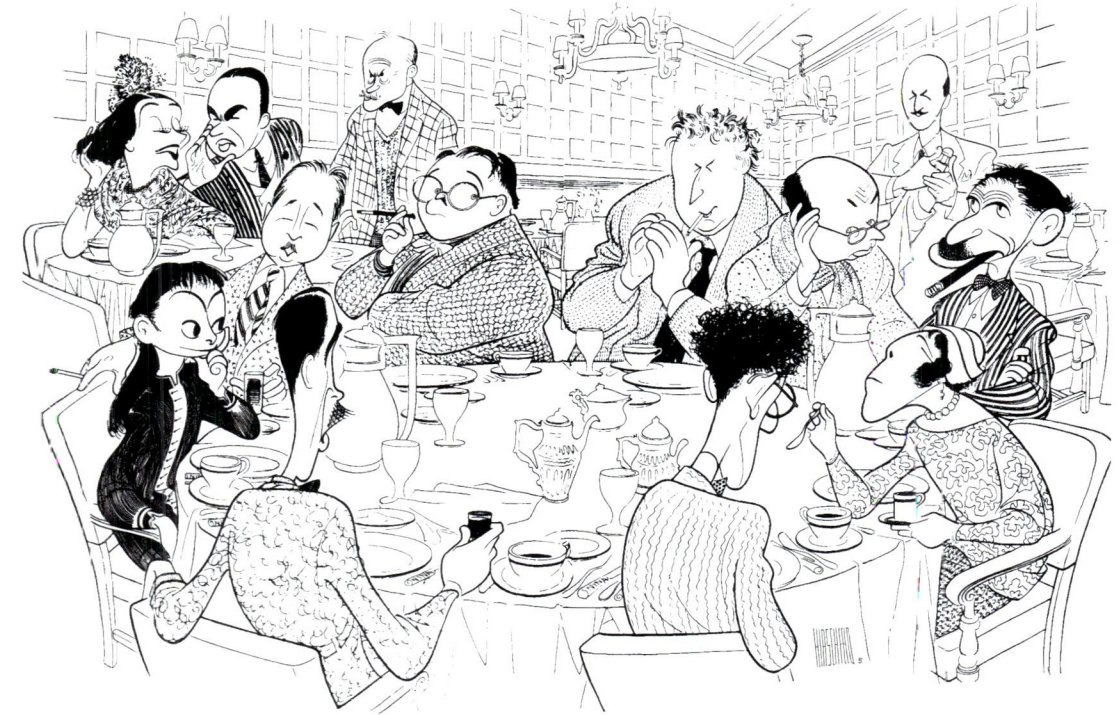

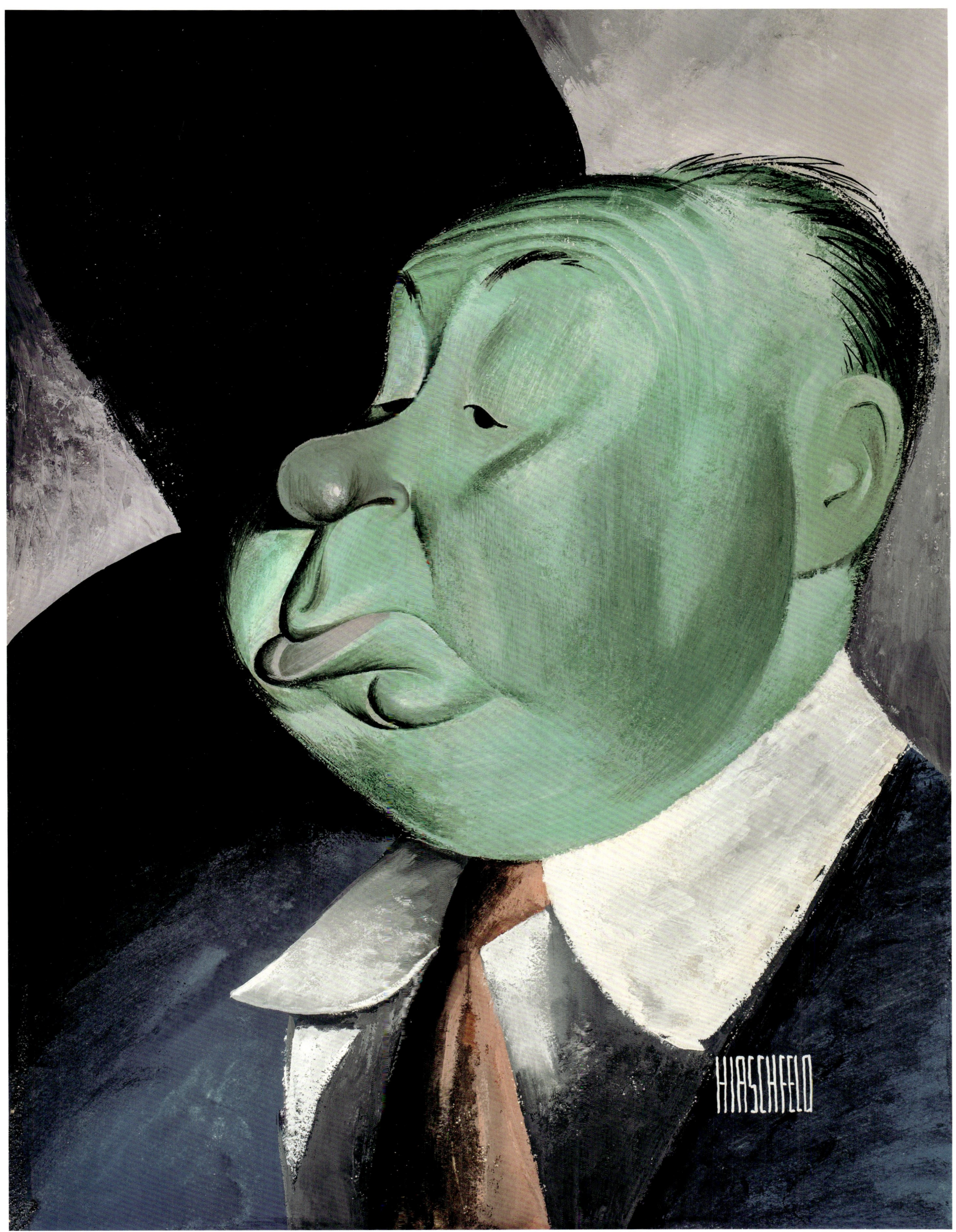

ALFRED HITCHCOCK

August 13, 1899–April 29, 1980

Gouache on board, 1957

TV Guide cover, November 30, 1957

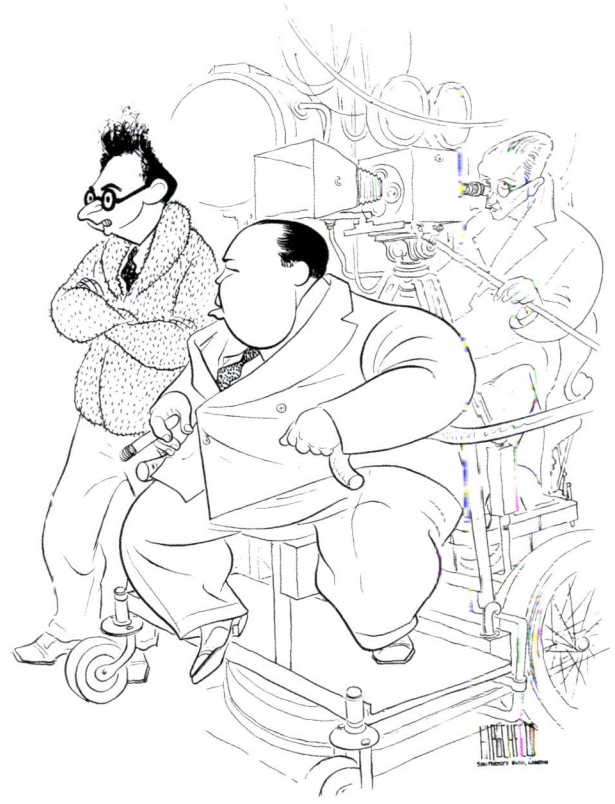

Alfred Hitchcock was an acclaimed film director who is considered among the most important figures in cinema history, with four films on the American Film Institute (AFI) list of 100 greatest American films of all time: *Psycho* (no. 18), *North by Northwest* (no. 40), *Rear Window* (no. 42), and *Vertigo* (no. 61). Often called the Master of Suspense, Hitchcock is widely credited with helping to shape thrillers for a modern audience. With a cameo in each of his films and his deadpan humor when introducing each episode of the television series *Alfred Hitchcock Presents* (1955–65), he became as well known an icon as many of the stars he directed.

Hitchcock claimed, "My suspense work comes out of creating nightmares for the audience. And I play with an audience. I make them gasp and surprise them and shock them. When you have a nightmare, it's awfully vivid if you're dreaming that you're being led to the electric chair. Then you're as happy as can be when you wake up, because you're relieved." The Hitchcock style frequently included the use of editing and camera movement to mimic a person's gaze, turning viewers into voyeurs and framing shots to amplify anxiety and fear.

Hirschfeld met Hitchcock in 1936 when the artist visited the London set of the film *Sabotage* (released in the United States in

1937 as *The Woman Alone*). Both RKO Pictures and United Artists used a Hirschfeld drawing of the director in their print ads for several of his films, including *Spellbound* (1945). The two men would meet again in 1952 when Hirschfeld's second wife, Dolly Haas, was cast in Hitchcock's *I Confess* (1953).

ABOVE

Alfred Hitchcock, 1936

The director with producer Ivor Montagu on the set of *Sabotage*

BELOW

CBS Friday Night, 1962

LEFT TO RIGHT: Van Heflin and characters from *The Great Adventure*; Martin Milner and Glenn Corbett in *Route 66*; Rod Serling in *The Twilight Zone*; Alfred Hitchcock in *Alfred Hitchcock Presents*, 1962

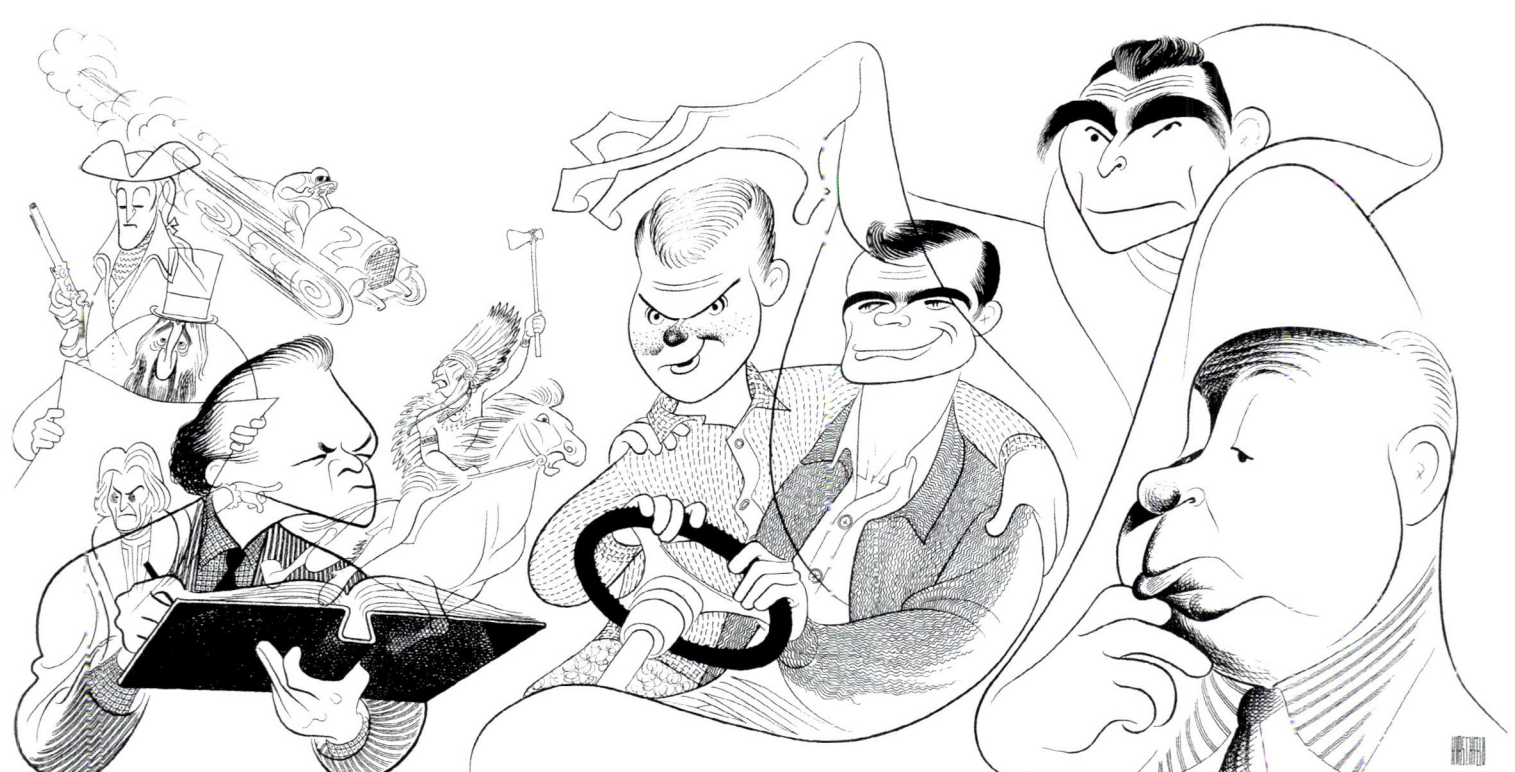

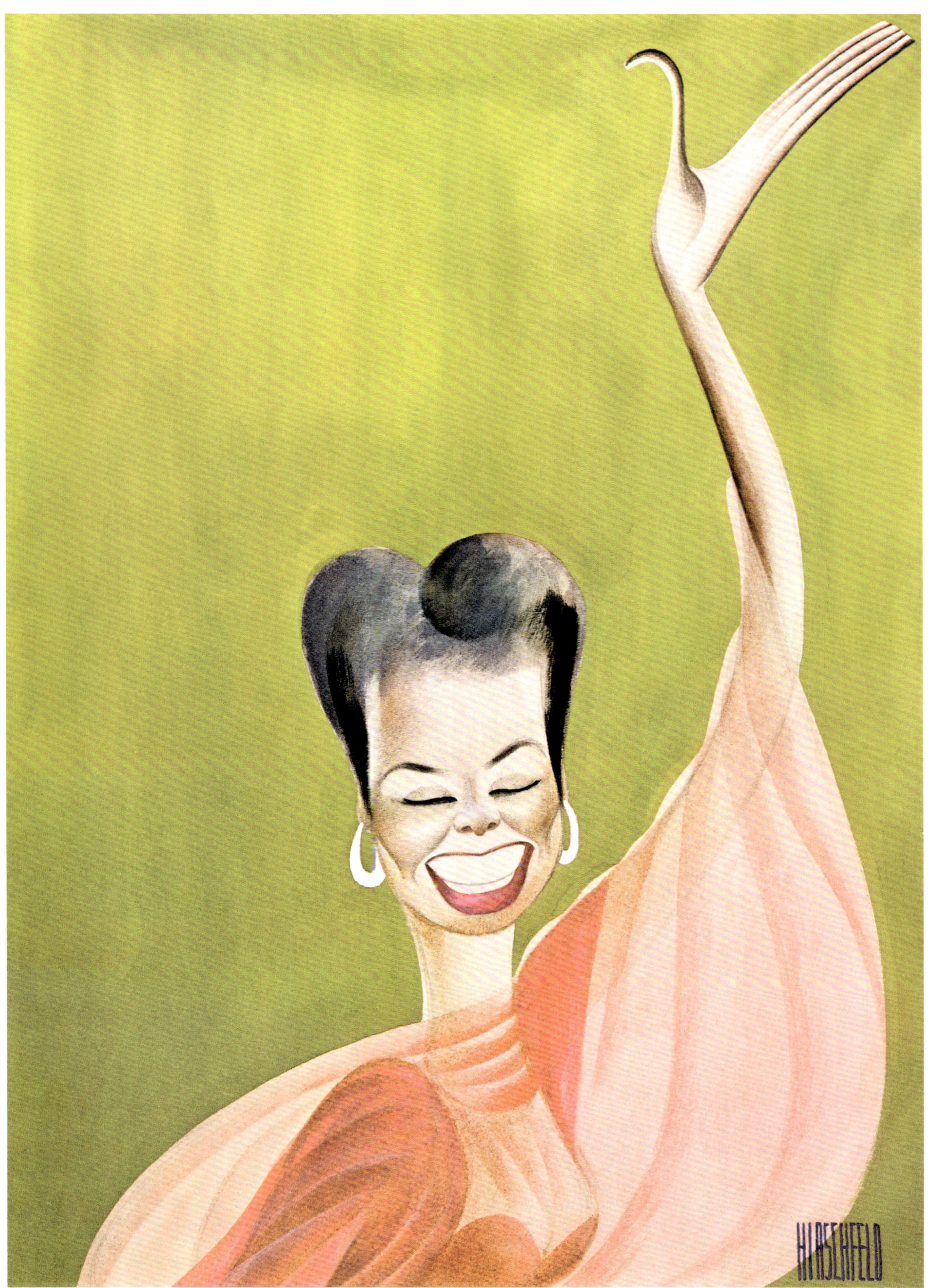

LENA HORNE

June 30, 1917–May 9, 2010

Gouache on board, c. 1950s

First publication unknown

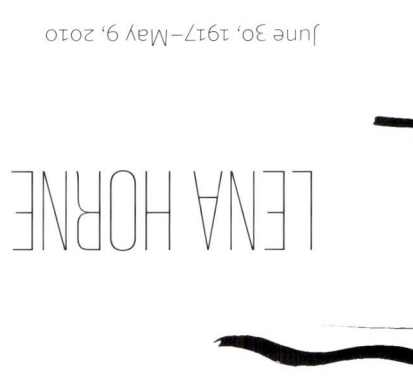

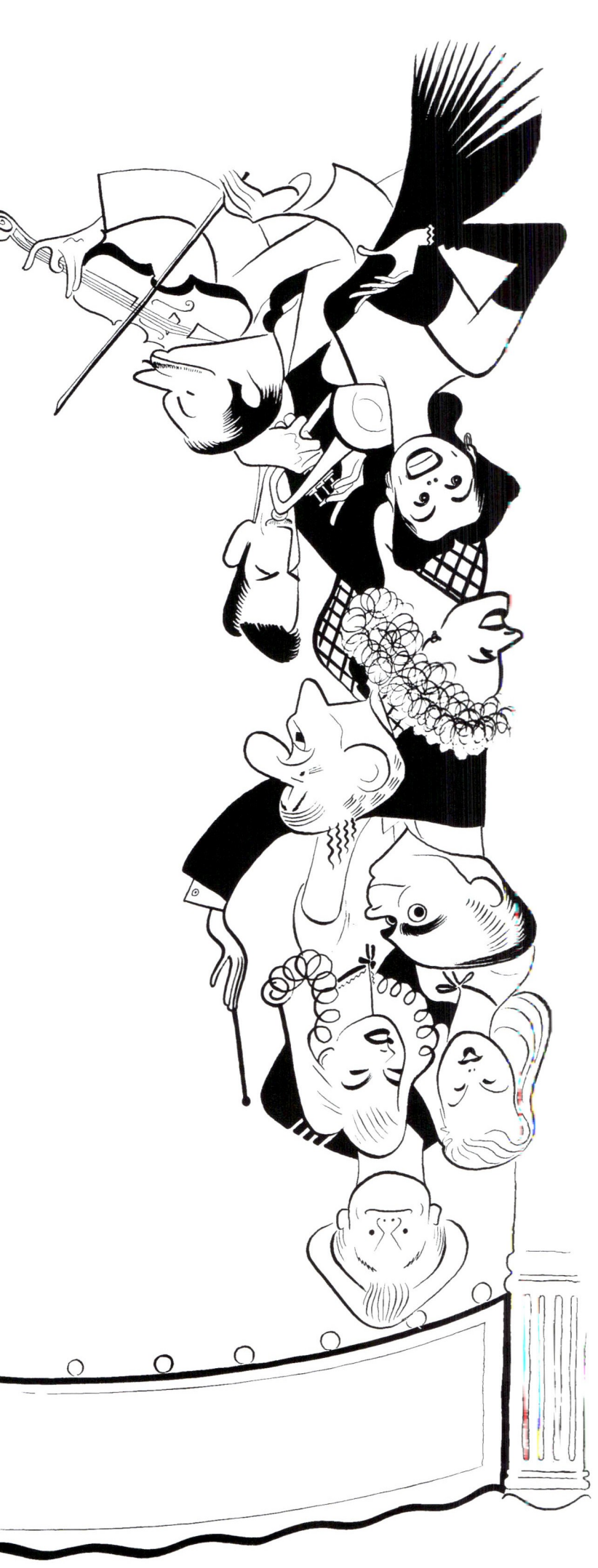

In a career that spanned more than seventy years in film, television, theater, and nightclubs, Lena Horne was an iconic singer, actress, dancer, and civil rights activist. As a Black performer in the predominantly white world of show business in mid-twentieth-century America, she refused stereotypical roles and fought for herself and other Black performers to be treated equally.

At the age of sixteen, Horne was in the chorus at Harlem's Cotton Club, later singing regularly at Café Society, the first integrated nightclub in New York. She left for a club in Los Angeles, but her goal was the movies. She and her father made it clear to MGM head Louis B. Mayer that she was not interested in playing maids. Horne appeared in a number of star-studded MGM films, including *Stormy Weather*, *Till the Clouds Roll By*, and *Ziegfeld Follies*, but her scenes were almost always solos so that they could be edited out for theaters in the South that refused to show scenes with Black performers to white audiences.

Horne was "tired of being typecast as a Negro who stands against a pillar singing a song. I did that twenty times too often." She returned to nightclubs and became one of the leading performers on that circuit in postwar America. Her *Lena Horne at the Waldorf-Astoria* album (1957) was a huge hit. In 1958, Horne became the first Black woman to be nominated for a Tony Award for Best Actress in a Musical for her role in *Jamaica*. At the March on Washington in 1963, she spoke and performed on behalf of the National Association for the Advancement of Colored People (NAACP), the Student Nonviolent Coordinating Committee (SNCC), and the National Council of Negro Women.

Hirschfeld was a regular at Café Society and certainly saw Horne sing there, but he first drew her for MGM and supplied the poster art for *Cabin in the Sky* (1943), the only all-Black film musical Horne was in at that studio. The two got to know each well when Hirschfeld's good friend, director Sidney Lumet, married Lena's daughter, Gail. His last drawings of Horne, more than fifty years after his first, were appropriately used on an album cover of her greatest hits released by RCA Victor in 2000.

LEFT
Two Girls and a Sailor, 1944
TOP TO BOTTOM: Van Johnson, June Allyson, Gloria DeHaven,
José Iturbi, Jimmy Durante, Gracie Allen, Harry James,
Xavier Cugat, and Lena Horne

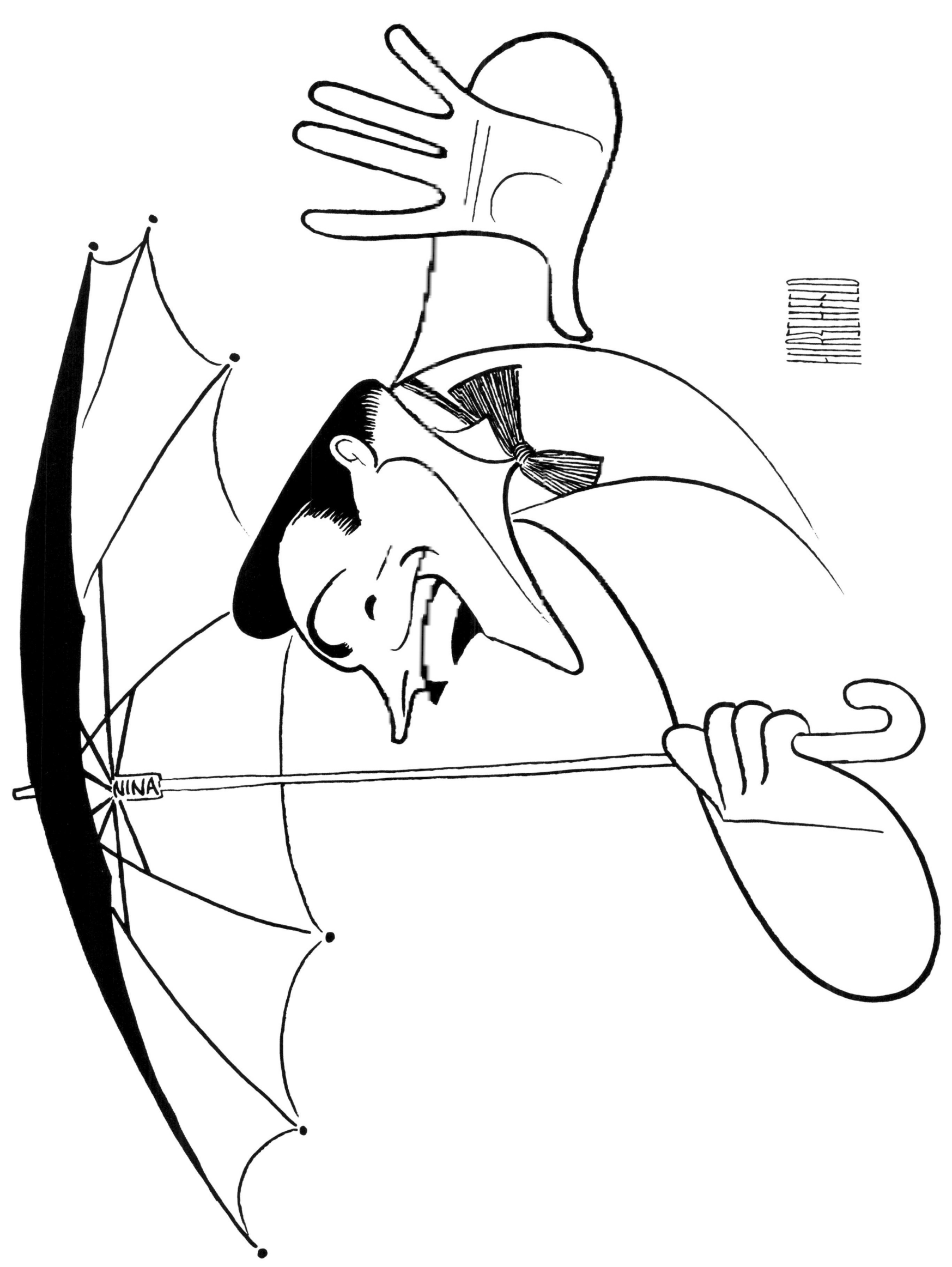

GENE KELLY

August 23, 1912–February 2, 1996

Ink on board, 1977

Advertisement for *Singin' in the Rain* on IBM's
Movies to Remember TV series, 1977

Singin' in the Rain, the romantic musical comedy written by Betty
Comden and Adolph Green and directed by Gene Kelly and Stan-
ley Donen about 1920s Hollywood, was a modest hit when it premiered in 1952. In a little more than a decade, it was seen as one of
the great films—musicals or otherwise—of Hollywood's Golden
Age. In 1989, *Singin' in the Rain* was one of the first twenty-
five films selected by the Library of Congress for preservation in
the National Film Registry for being "culturally, historically, or
aesthetically significant."

Hirschfeld distinctly summarizes the feeling and personality
of the 103-minute film in a single drawing, pared to its essential lines. This image, drawn on a board no bigger than 16 by 20
inches, captures 9,270 feet of film.

Hirschfeld's first drawing of *Singin' in the Rain* was created for MGM's publicity campaign when the movie was first

released. It is a busier drawing than this later one from 1977,
and includes the three leads—Gene Kelly, Debbie Reynolds, and
Donald O'Connor—against a backdrop of showgirls and cur-
tains that captures the characters and the film's exuberance. This
image was sent to publications around the world and appeared
everywhere. One of the secrets to Hirschfeld drawings is that
they require no translation, because even without the title or the
performers being named, he telescopes the kind of movie the
depicted film is.

Twenty-five years after Hirschfeld's initial image of the film,
he was asked to draw it again for a special television presenta-
tion. By this time, Hirschfeld only had to present the now-iconic
image of Kelly holding an umbrella for audiences to instantly
recognize not just the movie, but the performer and the song
as well.

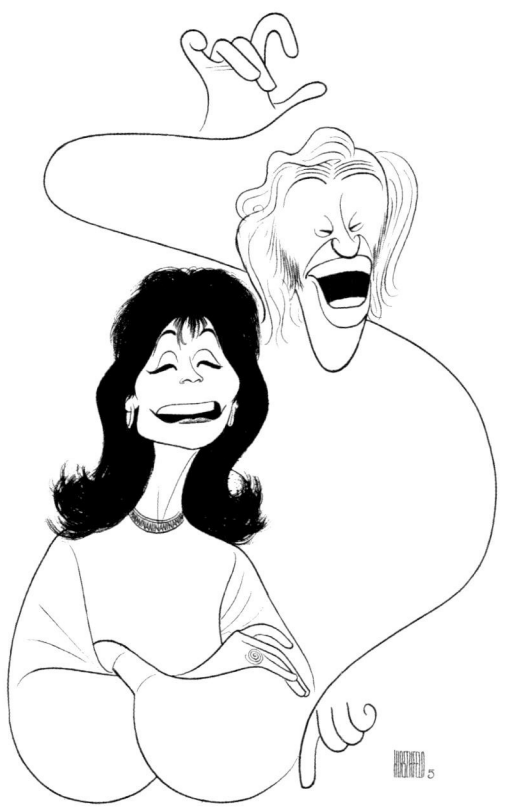

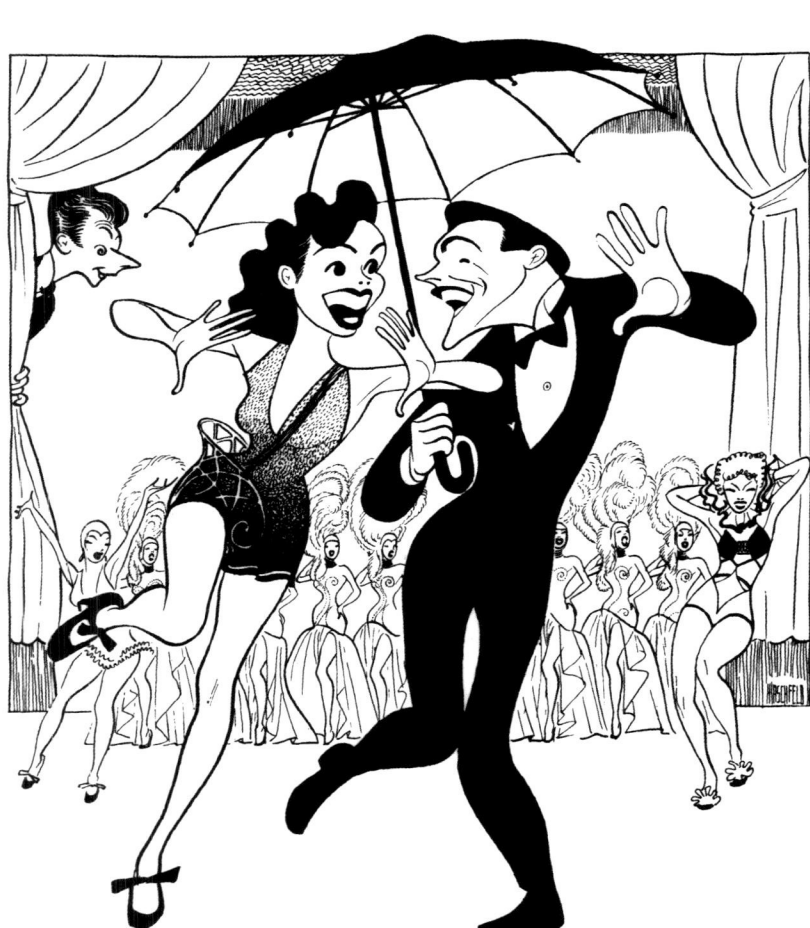

ABOVE

Betty Comden and Adolph Green, 1977

This songwriting duo wrote the screenplay for
Singin' in the Rain, as well as dozens of other hit
movies and Broadway shows.

LEFT

Singin' in the Rain, 1952

Donald O'Connor, Debbie Reynolds, Gene Kelly,
and Jean Hagen

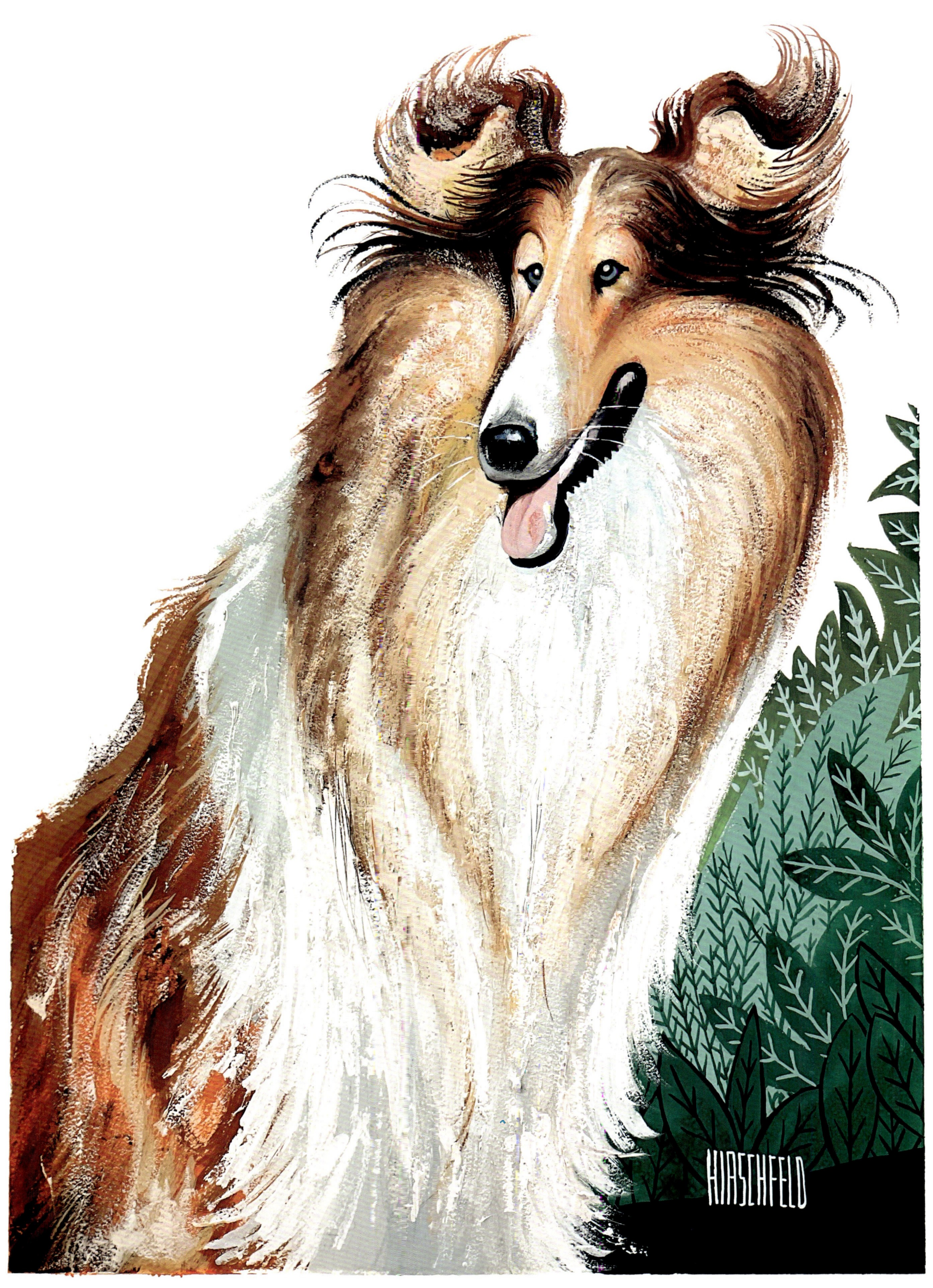

LASSIE

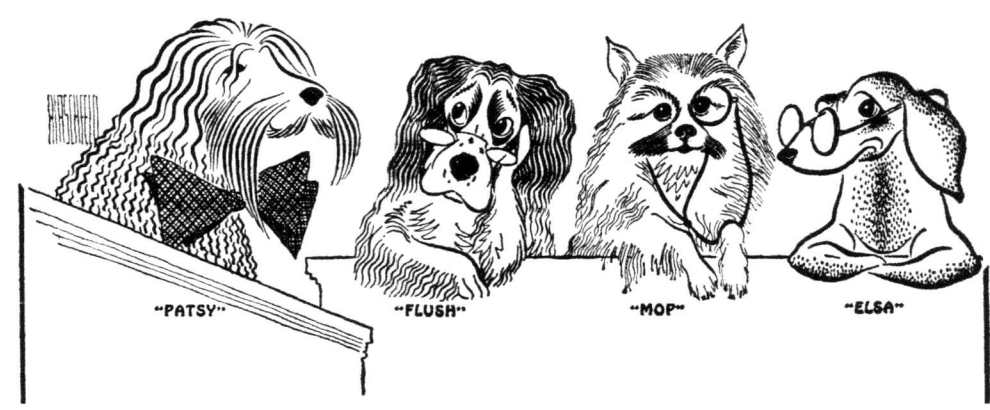

June 4 1940–June 18, 1958

Gouache on board, 1958

TV Guide cover, March 1, 1958
(shown here in full for the first time)

Hirschfeld went to the dogs early in his career. He drew publicity images of Rin Tin Tin in the 1920s, along with other film star canines, Flash and Strongheart. In the 1930s, he drew for Broadway's *Storm Over Patsy*, a comedy about a woman who is unable to afford a new "dog tax" and risks losing her dog, Patsy, before a reporter takes up her case and saves the day (and Patsy). Hirschfeld drew Patsy for two newspapers and eventually drew an ad for the show that featured the dogs of several actresses opining about the show.

In 1938, Eric Knight published a short story about a collie named Lassie. He later expanded the story into a novel, *Lassie Come-Home*, and an icon was born. MGM made seven films starring "Lassie," a collie whose offscreen name was Pal. Pal and his descendants have appeared in radio, film, comic books, animated series, young adult novels, and other media. In 1954, Lassie came to every home with a television, and for the next nineteen years she and her human companions rescued themselves and other people in weekly episodes, putting the show

in the top ten of the longest-running scripted American prime-time television series. Lassie was the first animal to get its own cover of *TV Guide*. With this illustration, Hirschfeld brought color to Lassie seven years before she was seen that way on TV.

ABOVE

Advertisement for *Storm Over Patsy*, 1937

This Broadway comedy was desperate to fill seats, so the Theatre Guild "awarded" the show the "Dog Critics Circle Award" and included Patsy, the show's star, alongside invented quotes from the pups of (left to right) Katharine Cornell, Helen Hayes, and Lynn Fontanne.

BELOW

CBS on Sunday, 1962

CLOCKWISE FROM TOP LEFT: Walter Cronkite; Ray Walston in *My Favorite Martian*; Judy Garland; Durward Kirby and Allen Funt in *Candid Camera*; John Daly, Arlene Francis, Bennett Cerf, and Dorothy Kilgallen in *What's My Line?*; Ed Sullivan; John Provost in *Lassie*; and Alan Young in *Mister Ed*

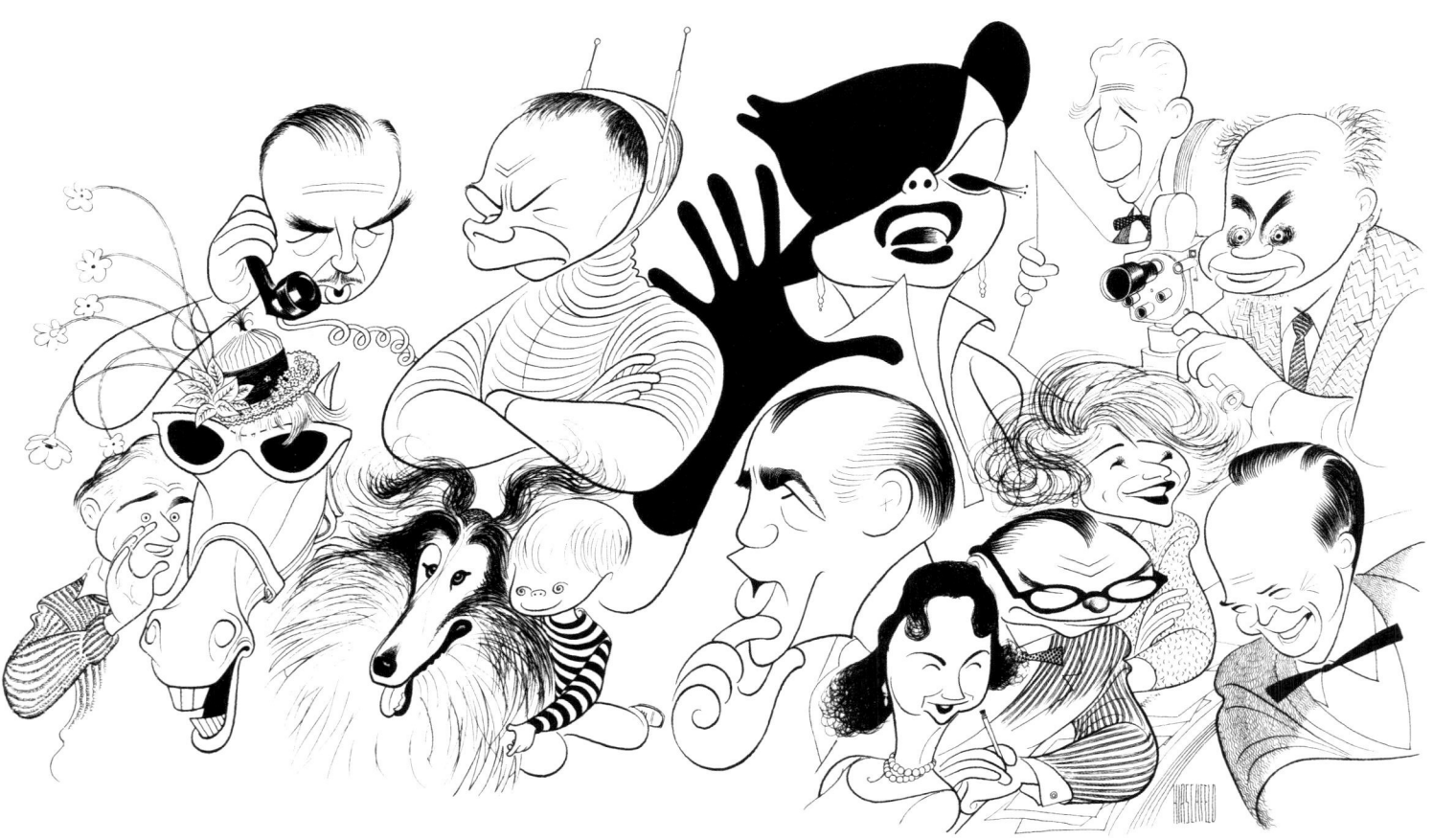

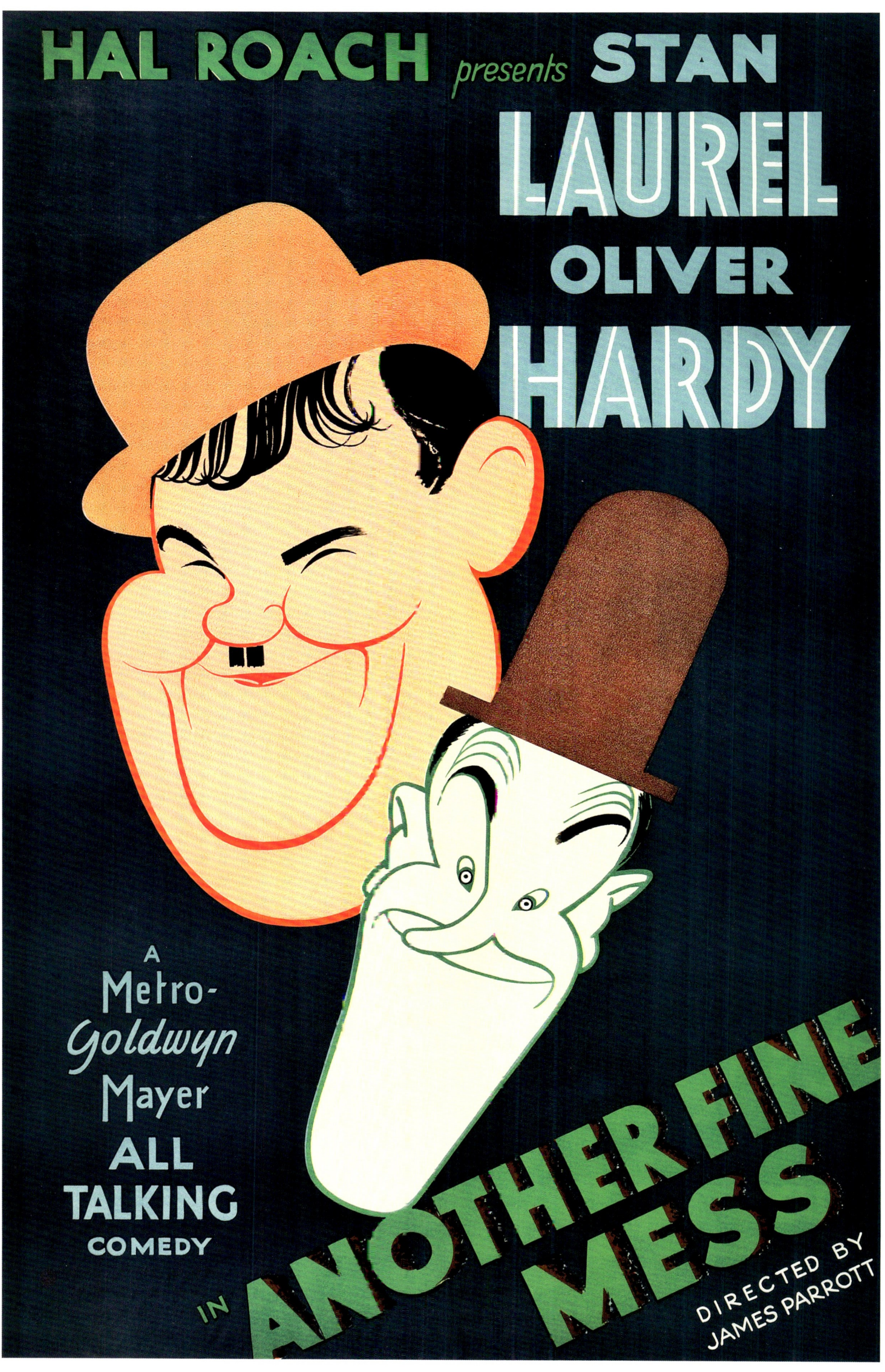

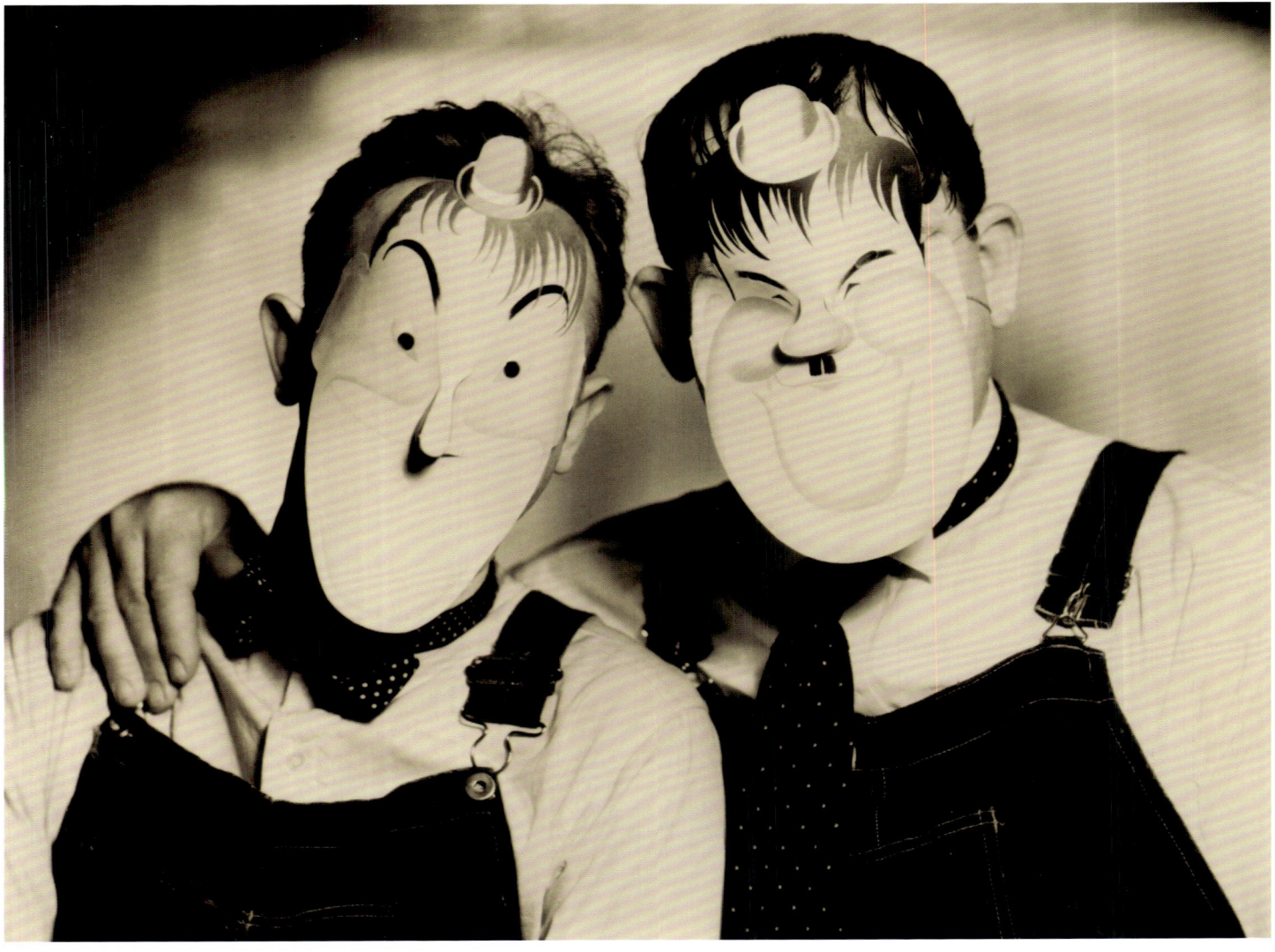

LAUREL and HARDY

ABCVE
Laurel and Hardy

The photograph shows the team wearing Hirschfeld-drawn masks that were offered to theater owners to promote Laurel and Hardy films, c. 1933.

Stan Laurel: June 16, 1890–February 23, 1965
Oliver Hardy: January 18, 1892–August 7, 1957

Another Fine Mess, stone lithograph poster, 1930

The comedy team of Stan Laurel and Oliver Hardy is considered among the funniest of all time, according to other comedians such as Abbott and Costello, Jerry Lewis, and Lucille Ball, as well as by writers Samuel Beckett, Kurt Vonnegut, and J. D. Salinger.

Although Laurel and Hardy debuted at the very end of the silent era, the team kept their slapstick humor primarily visual over the decades. In more than one hundred films—including the perennial classic *March of the Wooden Soldiers* (originally released as *Babes in Toyland* in 1934)—their humor required no translation to audiences around the world. It also made them a natural fit for Hirschfeld, who found character in movement and expression and could confidently translate those characteristics into line. Hirschfeld created almost all the posters and much of the black-and-white publicity art for their first eight feature films. His work was also recycled for many of the publicity campaigns for their film shorts. He would draw the duo at least eighty-seven times, more than any other performers.

This was the age of the great film poster, which is where Hirschfeld came into his own as an artist and really became *Hirschfeld*. A poster—the image in front of a theater—had to be rendered as simply as possible, with any extraneous detail eliminated, so its message could be immediately transmitted to passersby, whereas an image in a newspaper was intended to be "read" and could include a profusion of detail.

Hirschfeld said that the iconic duo looked like the number 10 to him, and his poster for *Another Fine Mess* (1930) distills the duo to two heads that were instantly recognizable to audiences. More people saw Hirschfeld's posters than would see the film itself in theaters, so Hirschfeld played a significant role in defining the image of Laurel and Hardy for the public.

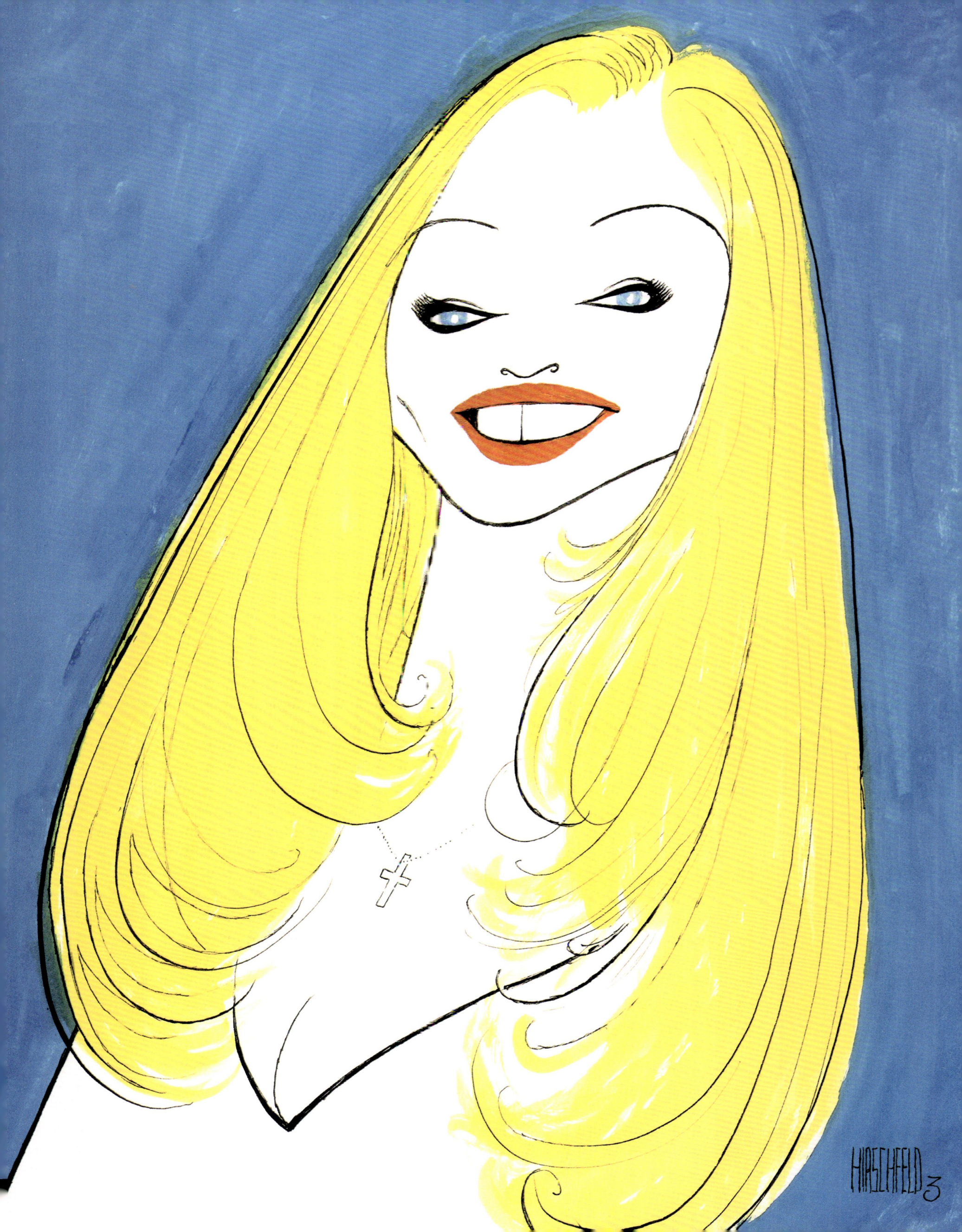

MADONNA

b. August 16, 1958

Ink and gouache on board, 1998

Rolling Stone, March 17, 1998

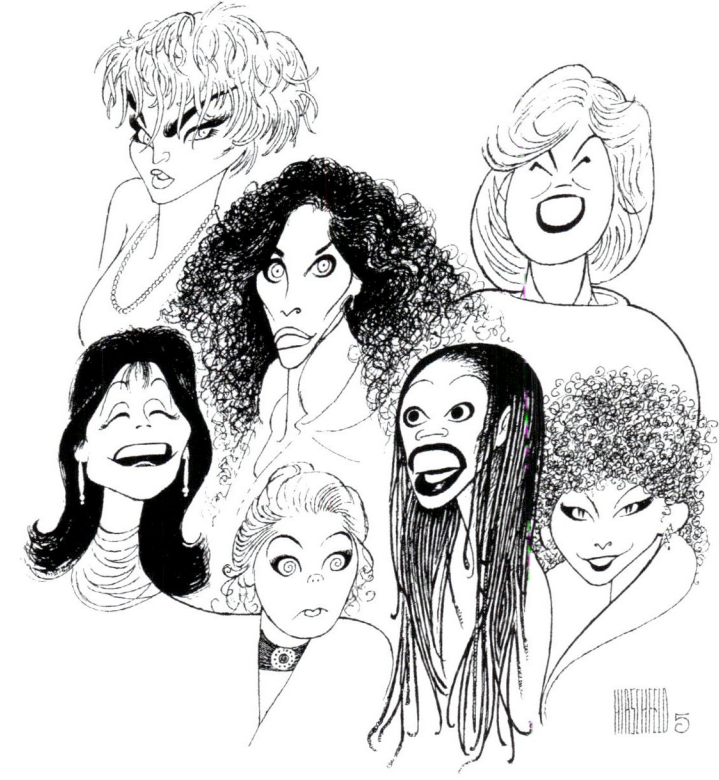

As an artist who clearly thinks about the image she is presenting, Madonna represents Hirschfeld's ideal subject to draw—an iconic performer who is larger than life with a personality to match. She is one of pop culture's great shapeshifters, and has reinvented herself and her conceptual approach to her music with each album release or tour. Hirschfeld understood and enjoyed capturing her metamorphosis. Before he first drew the Material Girl for *People* magazine in 1985, for decades he had been drawing performers who took on new roles and looks annually on Broadway and in Hollywood.

In 1986, Hirschfeld captured her "Papa Don't Preach" look in a drawing of the "Seven Women of ASCAP" (American Society of Composers, Authors and Publishers), showcasing her alongside other successful female writers, including Betty Comden and Carole King. Madonna has sold more than three hundred million records worldwide and is among the world's best-selling recording artists of all time.

Hirschfeld drew highlights of Madonna's next two decades: her Broadway debut in *Speed-the-Plow*, the David Mamet play from 1988; her Blond Ambition Tour in 1990; and, for the front page of the *New York Times* Arts & Leisure section, a dark-eyed and sultry pose in her *Sex/Erotica* phase on October 23, 1994.

This portrait appeared as a full page accompanying *Rolling Stone*'s review of her 1998 album *Ray of Light*, which some—including Madonna—consider her magnum opus. Her look was free of the studied artifice of her previous incarnations, and Hirschfeld captures the essence of an artist at the height of her powers in a few lines to suggest her features, with color added for detail and contrast.

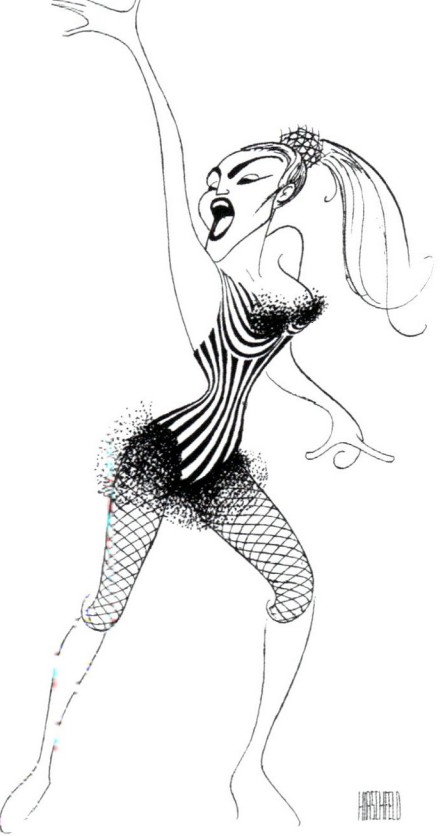

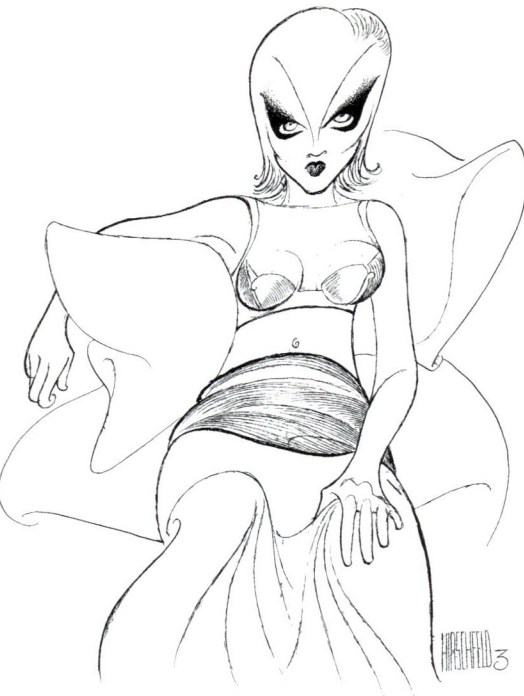

ABOVE

"Seven Women of ASCAP," 1986

CLOCKWISE FROM BOTTOM LEFT:
Betty Comden, Madonna,
Gloria Gaither, Carole King,
Reba McEntire, Valerie Simpson,
and Marilyn Bergman

FAR LEFT

Madonna, 1992

Showing the star costumed for
her Blond Ambition world tour,
this work was published as a
limited-edition lithograph.

LEFT

Madonna, 1994

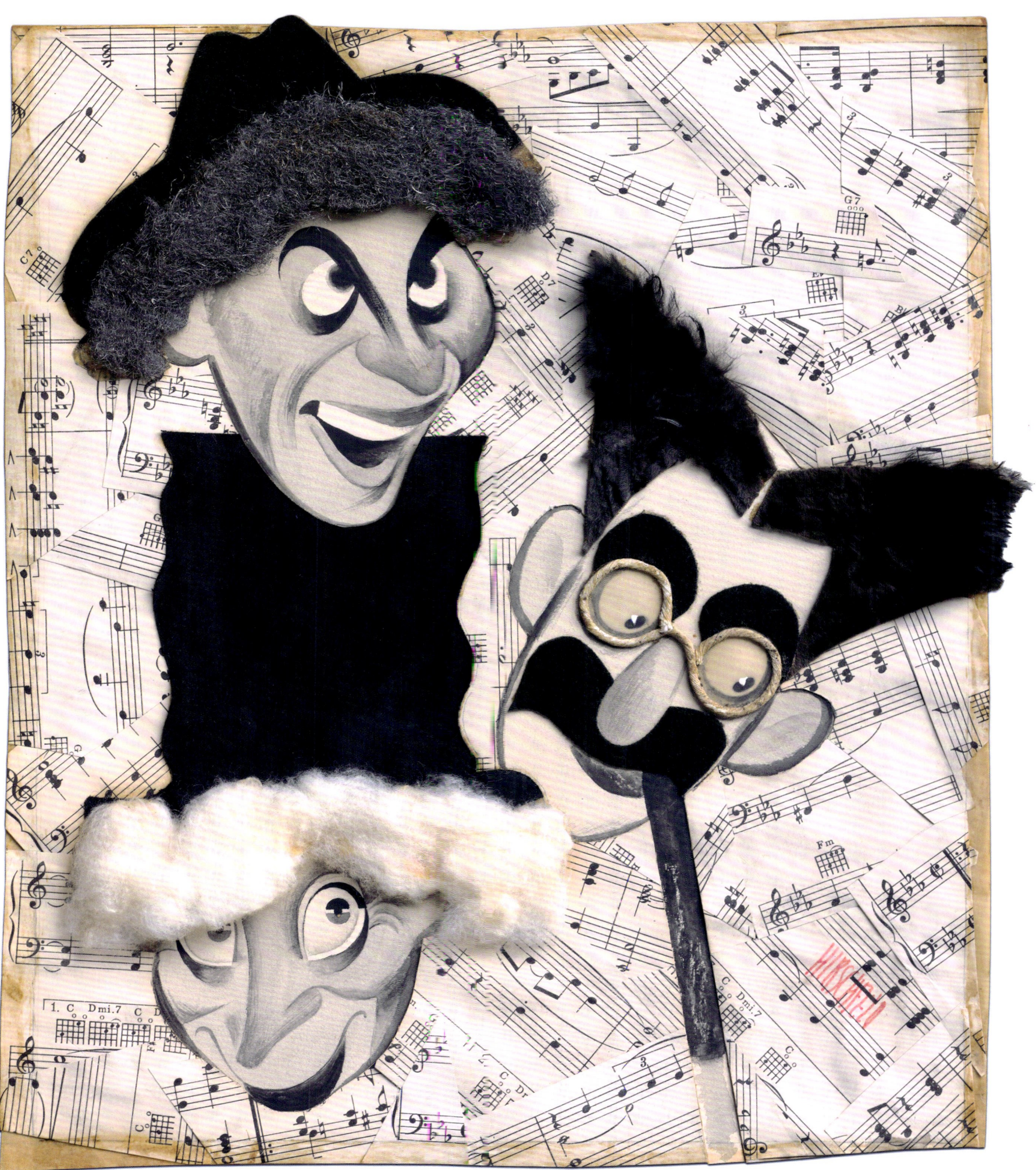

THE MARX BROTHERS

Chico (Leonard) Marx: March 22, 1887–October 11, 1961
Groucho (Julius) Marx: October 2, 1890–August 19, 1977
Harpo (Adolph, later Arthur) Marx: November 23, 1888–
September 28, 1964

Ink and opaque white, collaged with sheet music, silk, felt,
fur, cotton, string, and steel wool on board, 1935

Promotional image for the MGM film *A Night at the Opera*, 1935

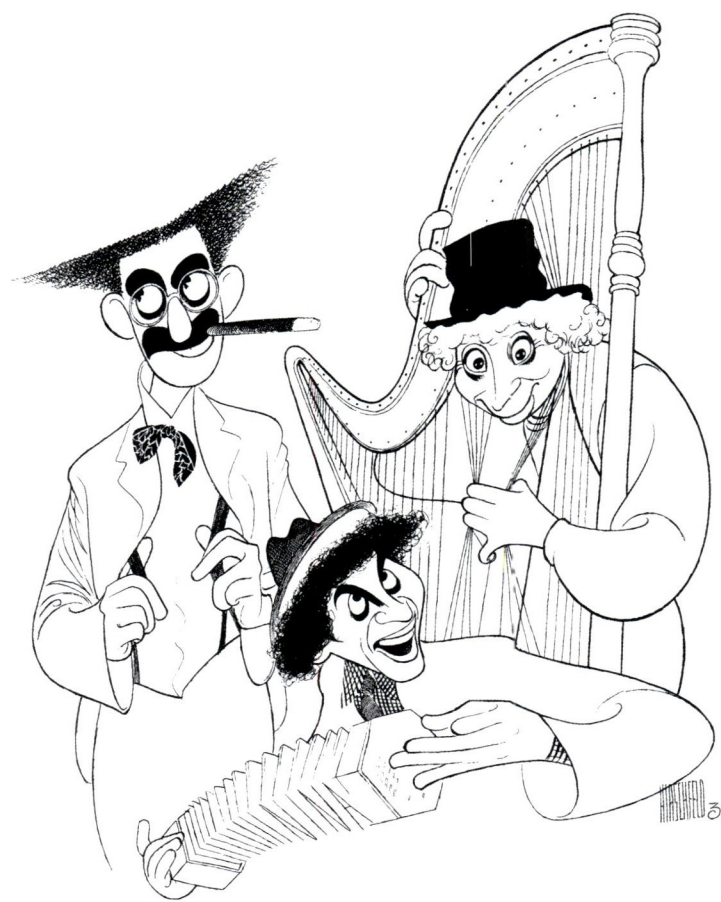

"I knew I was getting good," Hirschfeld once remarked, "when people started to look like my drawings, rather than the other way around." The iconic comedy trio the Marx Brothers were living proof of this statement. The team had been in vaudeville for twenty-five years and appeared in five feature-length films for Paramount before Hirschfeld got a crack at illustrating them. They had been drawn many times by many artists over the years, yet after Hirschfeld drew them in *A Night at the Opera* for MGM in 1935, not only did every subsequent drawing by pretty much every other artist look like Hirschfeld's image of them, but the Marx Brothers themselves tried to live up to their depiction in Hirschfeld's portraits. In their second film for MGM, *A Day at the Races* (1937), the costume department even tried to get Groucho's hair to be more like the two triangles that Hirschfeld had given him.

Hirschfeld's collage of the Marxes is a great example of how Hirschfeld saw his subjects. When sketching a performance, Hirschfeld drew what the performers looked like, but he also included words to remind him what the performance felt like. For a performer with kinky hair, he might write "Brillo Pad" next to the head, or next to a buxom actress he would write "behind on front." In this collage, he literally gave Chico steel wool for hair; for Harpo, cotton balls to simulate his wig; and for Groucho, a wide felt mustache and string for glasses, all of which brought Hirschfeld's descriptions to life.

The original of this collage is part of the permanent collection of the National Portrait Gallery in Washington, DC, and was purchased from Hirschfeld in 1992. It was later the signature image for their landmark 1998 exhibition *Celebrity Caricature in America*, and the cover of the companion book.

ABOVE
The Marx Brothers, 1989
This classic image was published as a limited-edition lithograph.

BELOW
A Day at the Races, 1937
This twenty-four-sheet poster image (printed at 108 x 246 inches) was one of six posters Hirschfeld contributed to the film's publicity campaign.

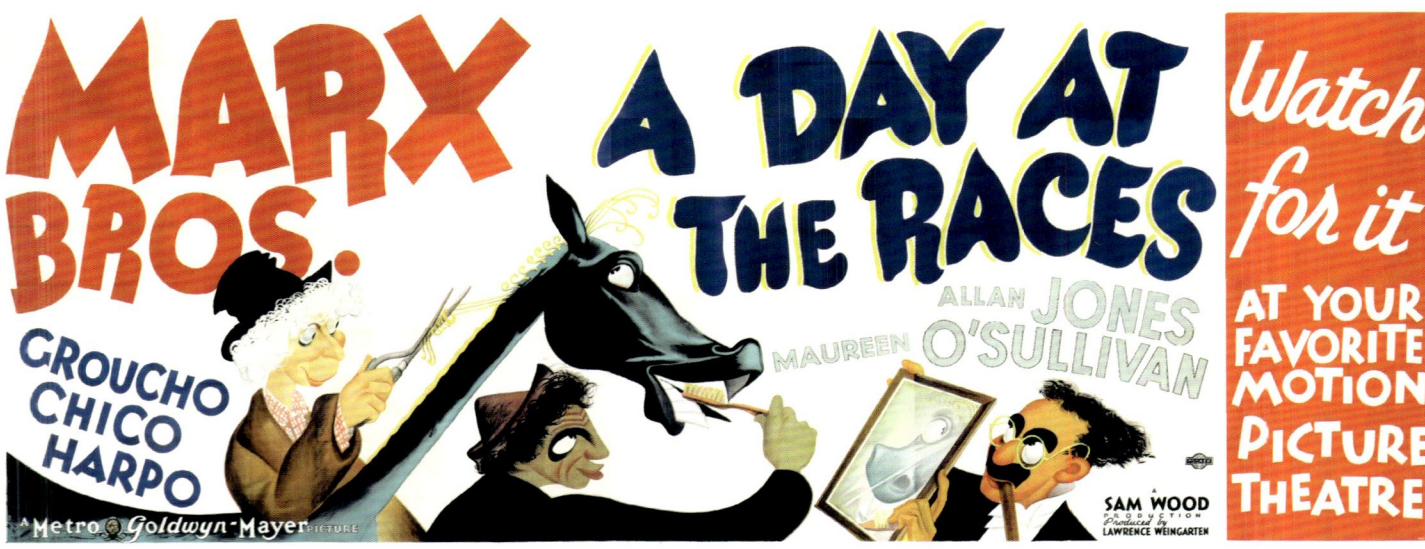

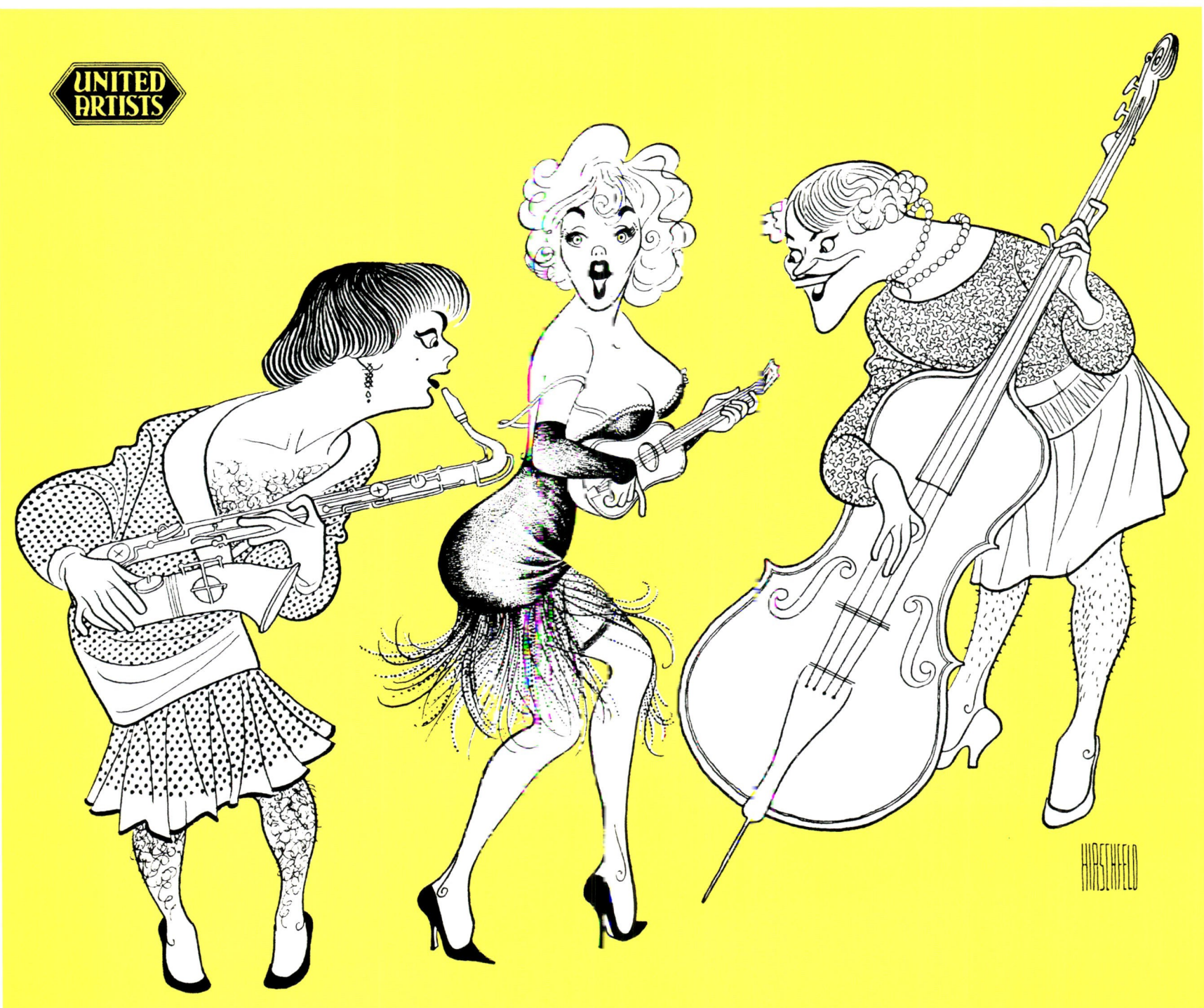

UNITED ARTISTS

HIRSCHFELD

MARILYN MONROE
TONY CURTIS · JACK LEMMON

in einer **BILLY WILDER** *Produktion*

MANCHE MÖGEN'S HEISS
SOME LIKE IT HOT

In weiteren Hauptrollen: GEORGE RAFT · PAT O'BRIEN · JOE E. BROWN
Drehbuch: BILLY WILDER *und* J. A. DIAMOND *Regie:* BILLY WILDER

Ein ASHTON *Film der* MIRISCH COMPANY

FSK

MARILYN MONROE

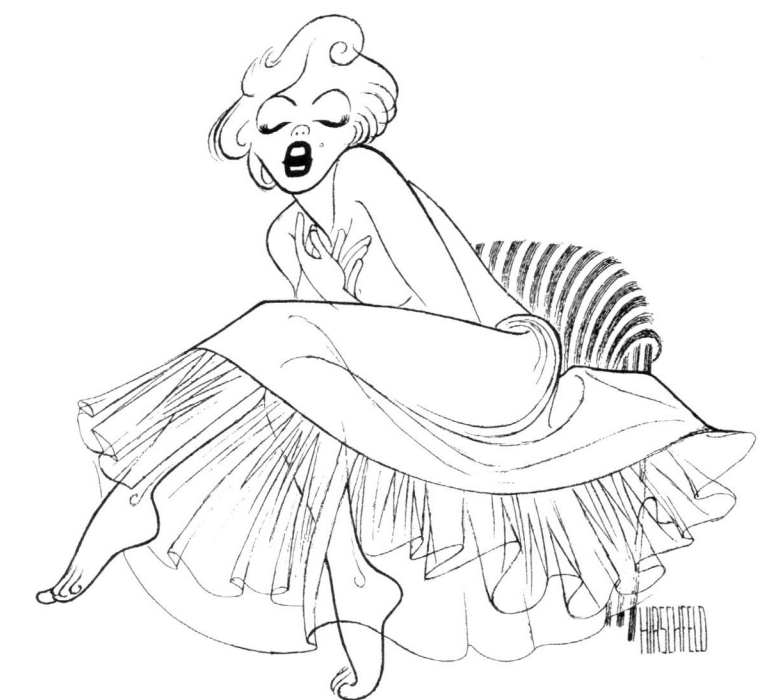

June 1, 1926–August 4, 1962

Offset lithograph, 1959

German poster for *Some Like It Hot* with Tony Curtis, Marilyn Monroe, and Jack Lemmon

International advertising campaign for *Some Like It Hot*, United Artists, 1959

One of Marilyn Monroe's many biographers described her as the embodiment of "the postwar ideal of the American girl: soft, transparently needy, worshipful of men, naive, offering sex without demands." Groucho Marx quipped that she was "Mae West, Theda Bara, and Bo Peep all rolled into one." For many, only Elvis and Mickey Mouse rank with Marilyn as a consummate American icon. Although often cast in the role of the "dumb blond," Marilyn was anything but that. It was she, not the studios, who had control of her image. Her longevity in popular culture has generated a spectrum of feelings from fans—from lust to pity, envy to remorse.

At first, Marilyn was not interested in what is considered one of her greatest roles. She was tired of playing the sex kitten, but, encouraged by her playwright husband, Arthur Miller, and a guarantee of 10 percent of the film's profits on top of her standard pay, she delivered a historic performance in *Some Like It Hot*, Billy Wilder's gender-bending comedy from 1959.

As the Hollywood studio system was breaking apart in the 1950s, Hirschfeld moved from MGM to United Artists, the biggest independent film distribution company. While the era of the great illustrated film poster was ending in America, the studio's publicity department understood that Hirschfeld's drawings had an audience of their own. His drawing for *Some Like It Hot* was sent to publications across the country. And in Germany, it was used as the film's poster image because it succinctly conveyed both the comedy and the tension of the film.

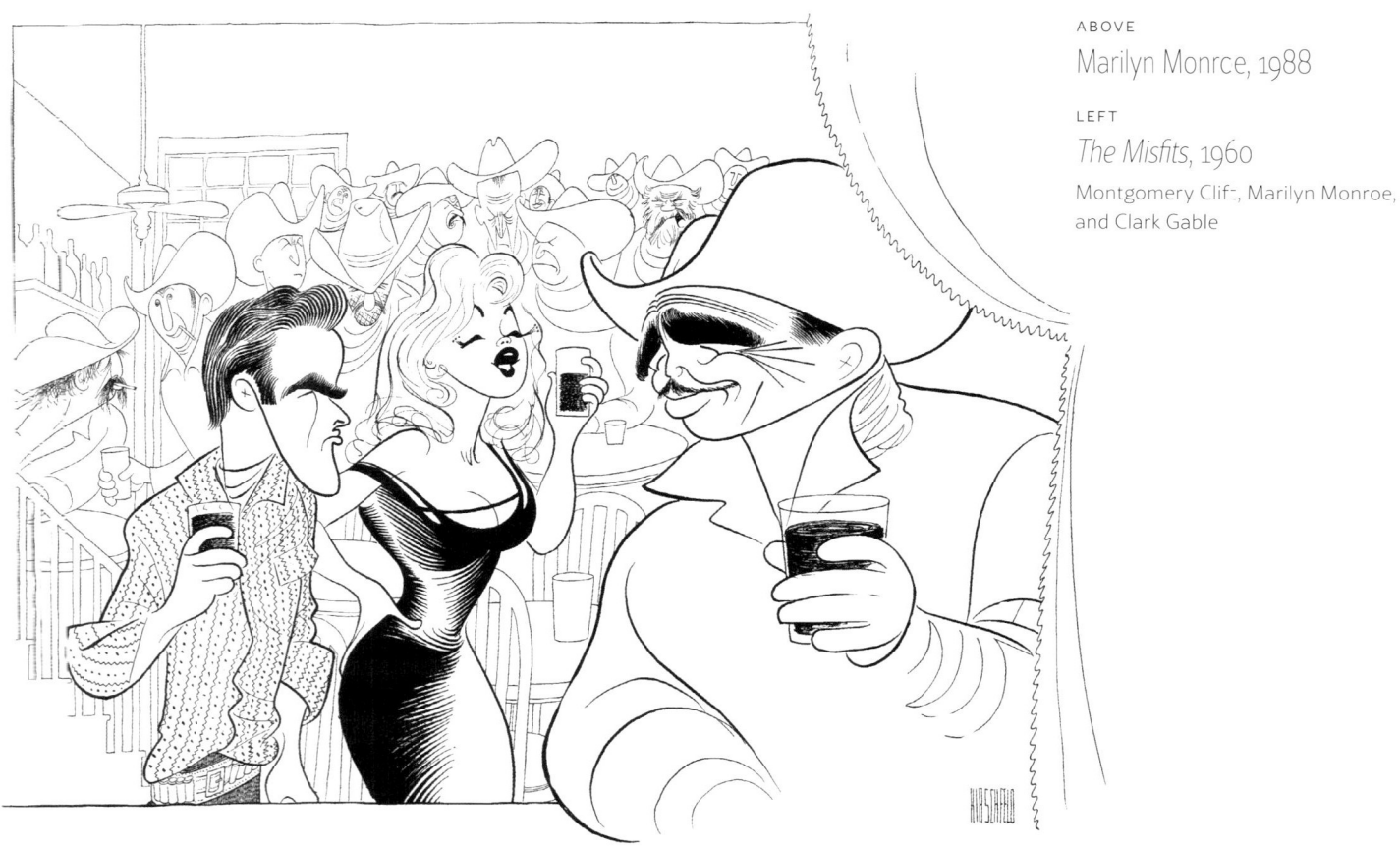

ABOVE
Marilyn Monroe, 1988

LEFT
The Misfits, 1960
Montgomery Clift, Marilyn Monroe, and Clark Gable

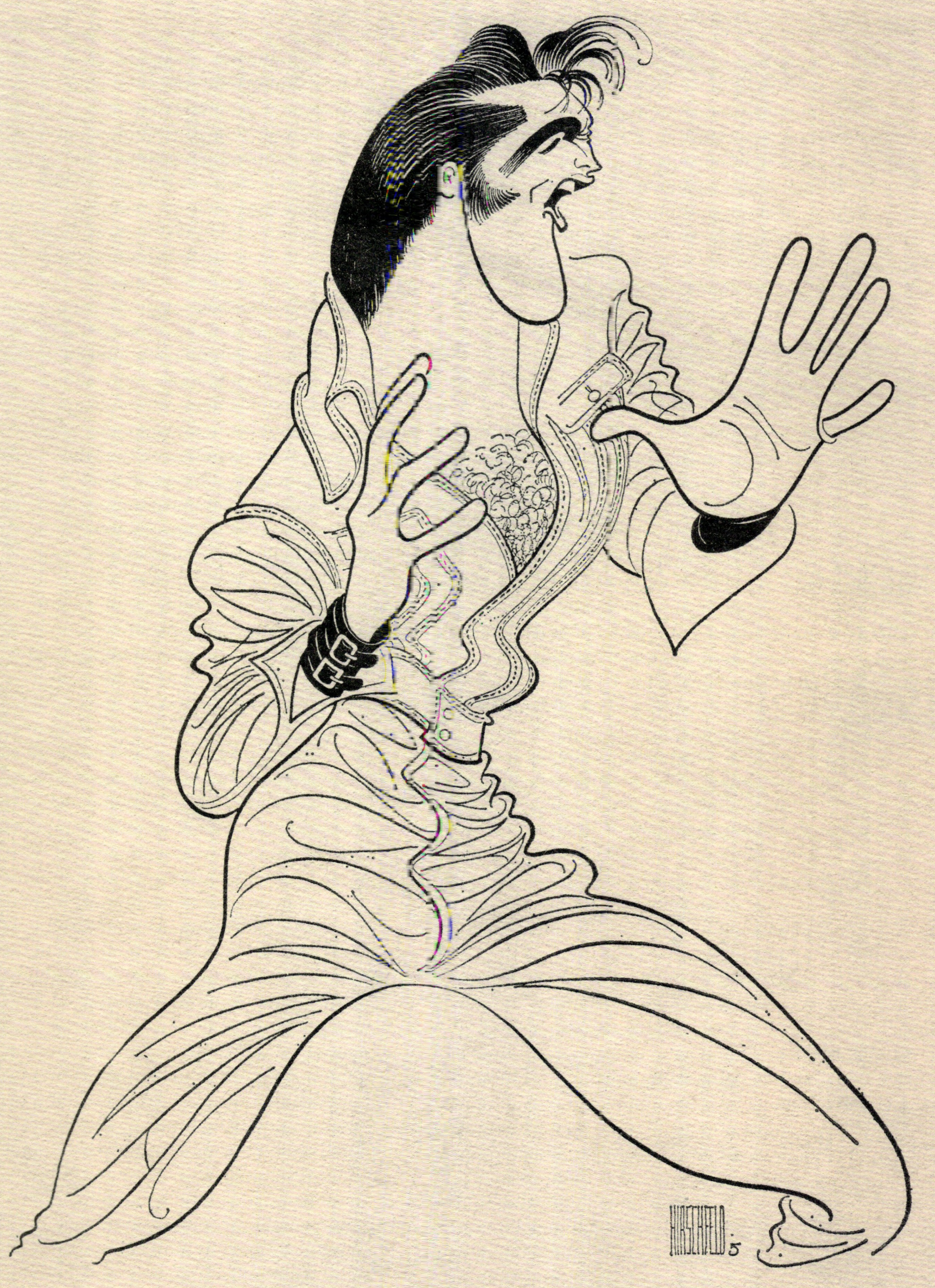

ELVIS PRESLEY

January 8, 1935–August 16, 1977

Newspaper clipping of ink on board drawing, 1968

The New York Times, December 1, 1968

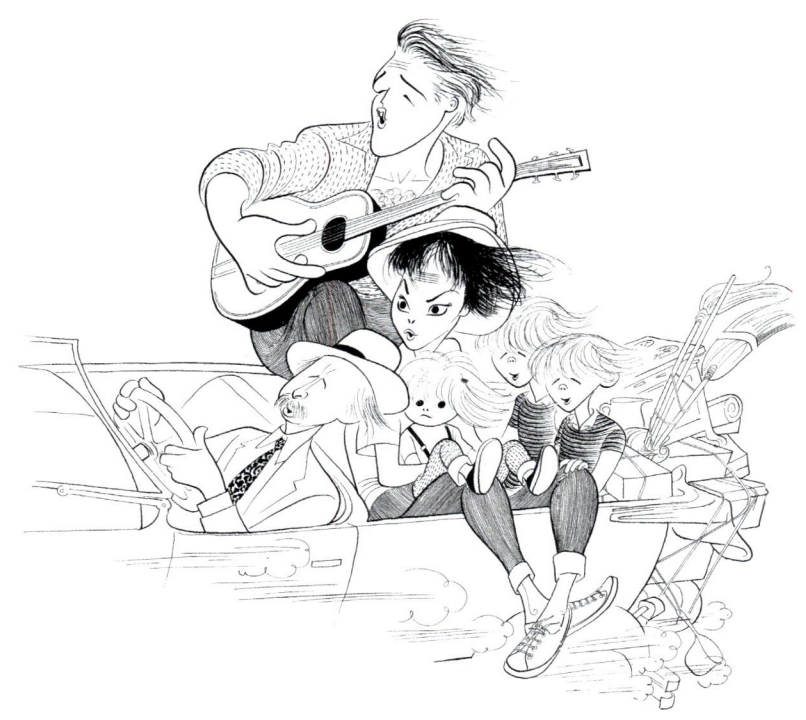

Bono claimed that Elvis Presley was the blueprint for rock and roll, and it turns out that Hirschfeld was on the ground floor. In 1956, he was the first to draw a caricature of Elvis, which ran in John O'Hara's column in *Collier's*. Although the "Line King" was fifty-three years old and not a rock and roll fan at the time, he couldn't seem to escape the King of Rock and Roll, as Elvis was becoming one of the most culturally important figures of the twentieth century. To date, he has sold over five hundred million records worldwide, expanding into the genres of country, gospel, and adult contemporary music.

Elvis, or a character based on Elvis being drafted into the army (played on stage by Dick Gautier), next shows up in a Hirschfeld drawing of the Broadway musical *Bye Bye Birdie* in 1960. Later that year, when Elvis returned from his military service overseas, he was greeted by a Hirschfeld advertisement in newspapers for a "Welcome Home Party" on television hosted by Frank Sinatra, the previous generation's pop star. Elvis had made his film debut in 1956 and spent most of the 1960s making movies including classics such as *Viva La Vegas* (1964), and many more that were soon forgotten. Hirschfeld was commissioned by United Artists in 1962 to create drawings to promote two of them, *Kid Galahad* and *Follow That Dream*.

It was therefore natural for Elvis's *'68 Comeback Special* on television to be heralded by this Hirschfeld drawing of Presley in his leather jumpsuit (in whose every crease seems to hide a NINA), accurately capturing the renewed vitality of the singer. This iconic image is the one Hirschfeld returned to repeatedly as the basis for future drawings of the singer.

ABOVE
Follow That Dream, 1962
Elvis Presley, Pam Ogles, Arthur O'Connell, Anne Helm, and Gavin and Robin Koon

BELOW, LEFT
Elvis Presley, 1956

BELOW, RIGHT
"Welcome Home Elvis," 1960
This advertisement ran in newspapers and other publications around the country, highlighting that the pop stars of two generations—Sinatra and Presley—would be performing side by side for the first time.

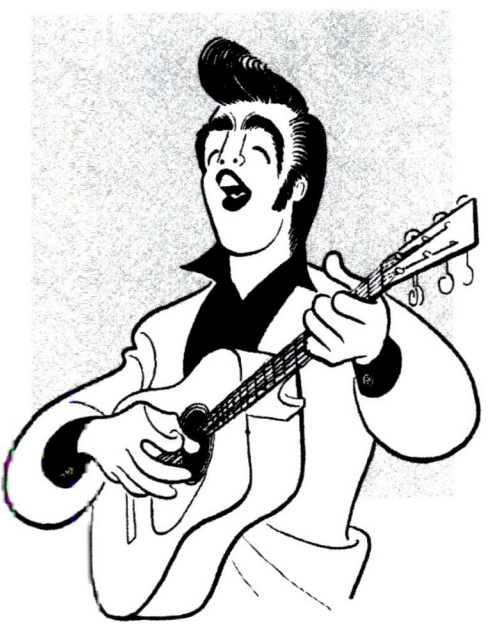

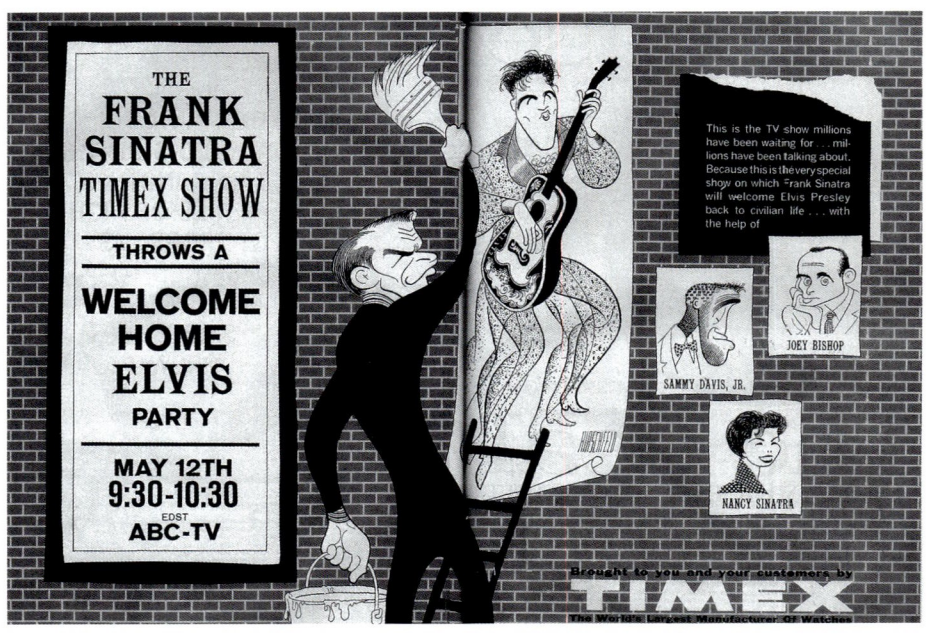

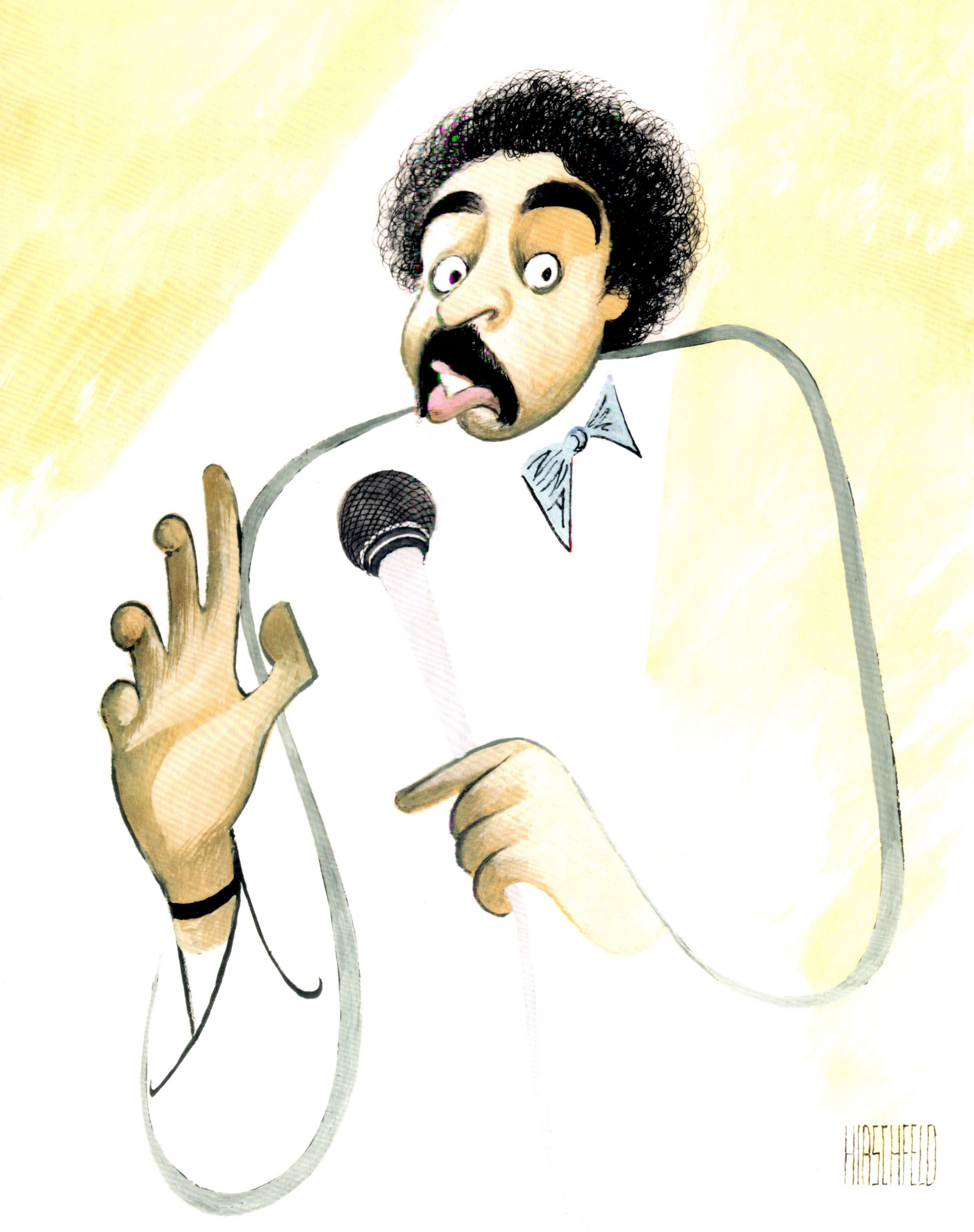

RICHARD PRYOR

December 1, 1940–December 10, 2005

Gouache on board, 1999

The New Yorker, September 13, 1999

Writer Larry Gelbart once described Al Hirschfeld working in his barber chair as a "sit-down comic," because humor was "constant in his work." Hirschfeld loved drawing comics. In his early days, comedians such as Will Rogers, Ed Wynn, Charlie Chaplin, and Buster Keaton, to name a few, came ready-made. As Hirschfeld would later say, "They looked like their caricatures." As comedy developed throughout the twentieth century, Hirschfeld was drawing right along with it, capturing comics like the Marx Brothers, Milton Berle, Imogene Coca, and Jerry Lewis all the way through the more modern performers of mid-century, like Woody Allen, Elaine May, Mike Nichols, and Lily Tomlin. Hirschfeld created film posters of Bob Hope, album covers for David Steinberg, advertisements for the Smothers Brothers,

TV Guide covers of Lucille Ball, and artwork for reviews in the magazine for programs like *The Phyllis Diller Show*. As the century closed, Hirschfeld continued to document comedians, with drawings of Sandra Bernhard, Whoopi Goldberg, John Leguizamo, Garry Shandling, and Tracey Ullman.

Jerry Seinfeld called Richard Pryor "the Picasso of our profession." Highly influential and always controversial, Pryor was a comedian, writer, and actor who was well known for his trenchant observations about race and relationships, his colorful storytelling style (often filled with racy language), and his fast-paced life, multiple marriages, and battles with drug addiction. Pryor is acknowledged by many modern comics as one of the greatest and most important stand-up comedians of all time.

Hirschfeld drew the icon in several film roles before he captured him in his natural environment: in the spotlight onstage. It is almost as if Pryor was making his famous observation, "What I'm saying might be profane, but it's also profound."

RIGHT

Tracey Ullman, 1997

As eleven different characters for her HBO series, *Tracey Takes On . . .*

BELOW

Ed Wynn in *The Chief*, 1933

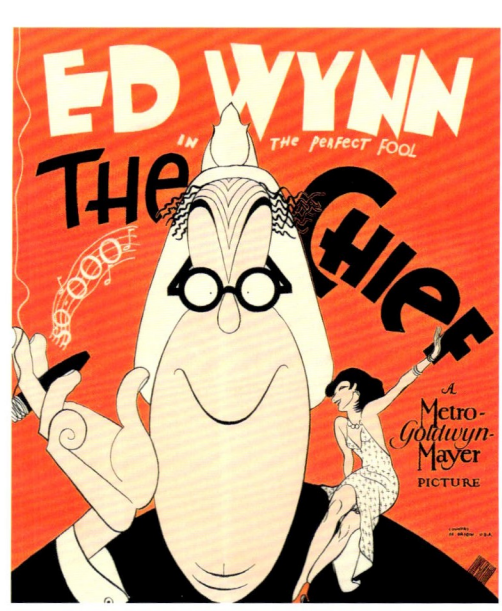

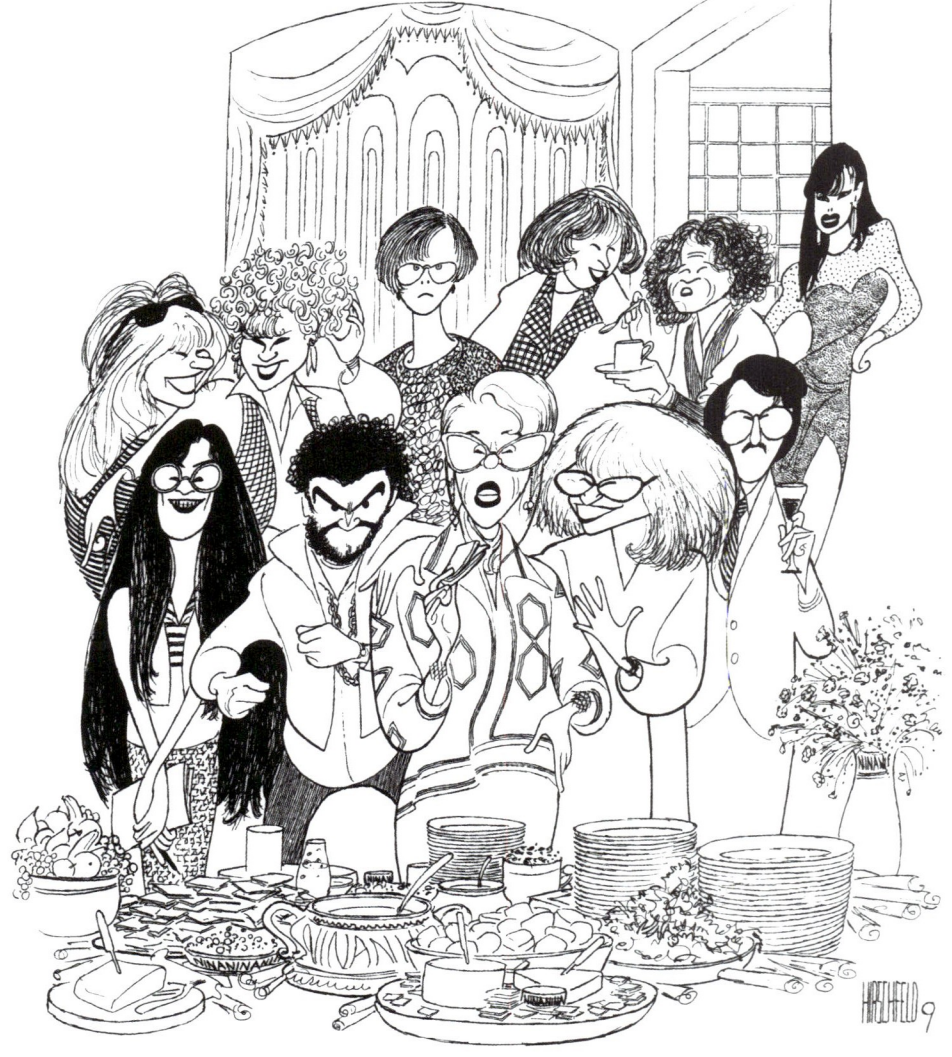

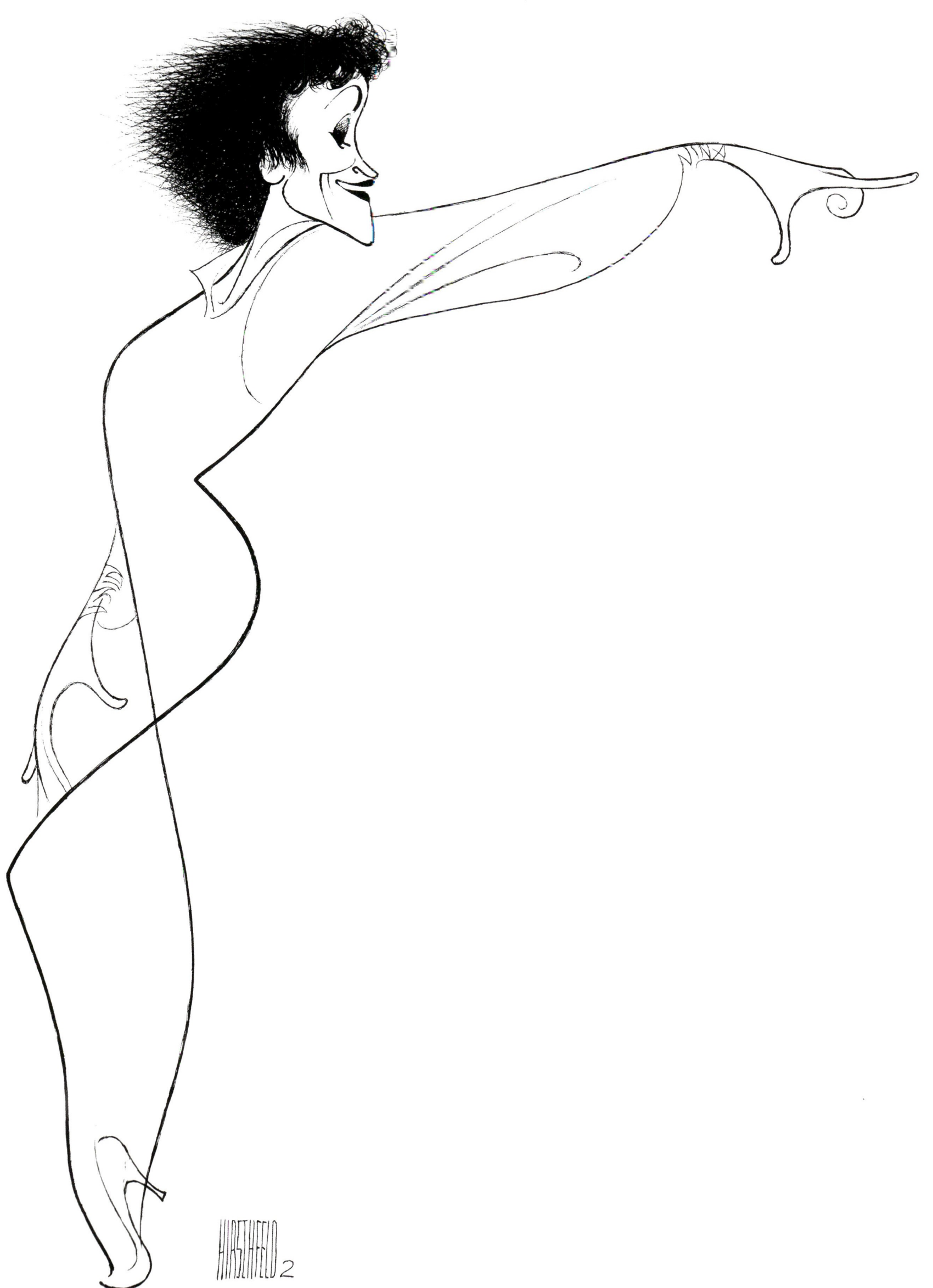

CHITA RIVERA

January 23, 1933–January 30, 2024

Ink on board, 1984

The New York Times, March 2, 1984.

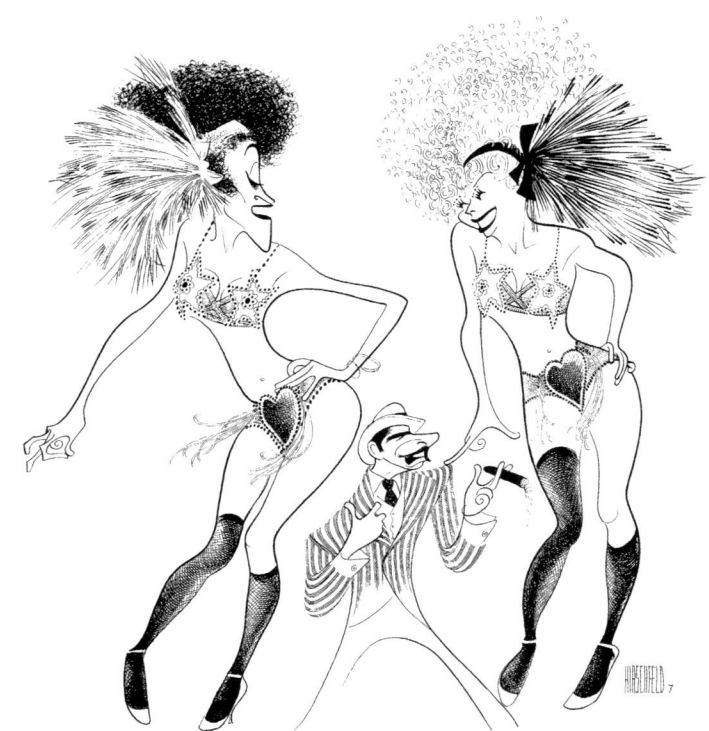

Chita Rivera was an American actress, singer, and, most of all, dancer. She starred on Broadway in such historic shows as *West Side Story*, *Bye Bye Birdie*, *Chicago*, and *Kiss of the Spider Woman*. Rivera was nominated a record ten times for Tony Awards as either Best Featured Actress in a Musical or Best Actress in a Musical. She was awarded two Tonys, two Drama Desk Awards, and a Drama League Award. She was the first Latino American to receive a Kennedy Center Honor in 2002 and the first to receive the Presidential Medal of Freedom in 2009. She also won a Tony Award for Lifetime Achievement in 2018. By anyone's definition, she is an icon.

Hirschfeld drew Rivera nine times before he received the assignment that led to this classic work in 1984. She was appearing in the Kander and Ebb musical *The Rink* with Liza Minnelli, a role for which Rivera won her first Tony. Hirschfeld reduced her body to two lines, yet they somehow reveal Rivera's athleticism, grace, movement, and beauty. When he finished this work, he told a friend, "I think I found a new way to draw."

Hirschfeld credited Mexican artist Miquel Covarrubias for introducing him to caricature. He started drawing Latino stars in the 1920s with portraits of Ramon Navarro, Dolores Del Rio, and Lupe Vélez. Throughout Hirschfeld's career, he captured performances by Jose Férrer, Anthony Quinn, Rita Moreno, Edward James Olmos, and John Leguizamo.

ABOVE
Chicago, 1975
LEFT TO RIGHT: Chita Rivera, Jerry Orbach, and Gwen Verdon
BELOW
Bye Bye Birdie, 1960
LEFT TO RIGHT: Dick Van Dyke, Dick Gautier, Susan Watson, Chita Rivera, Kay Medford, and Paul Lynde

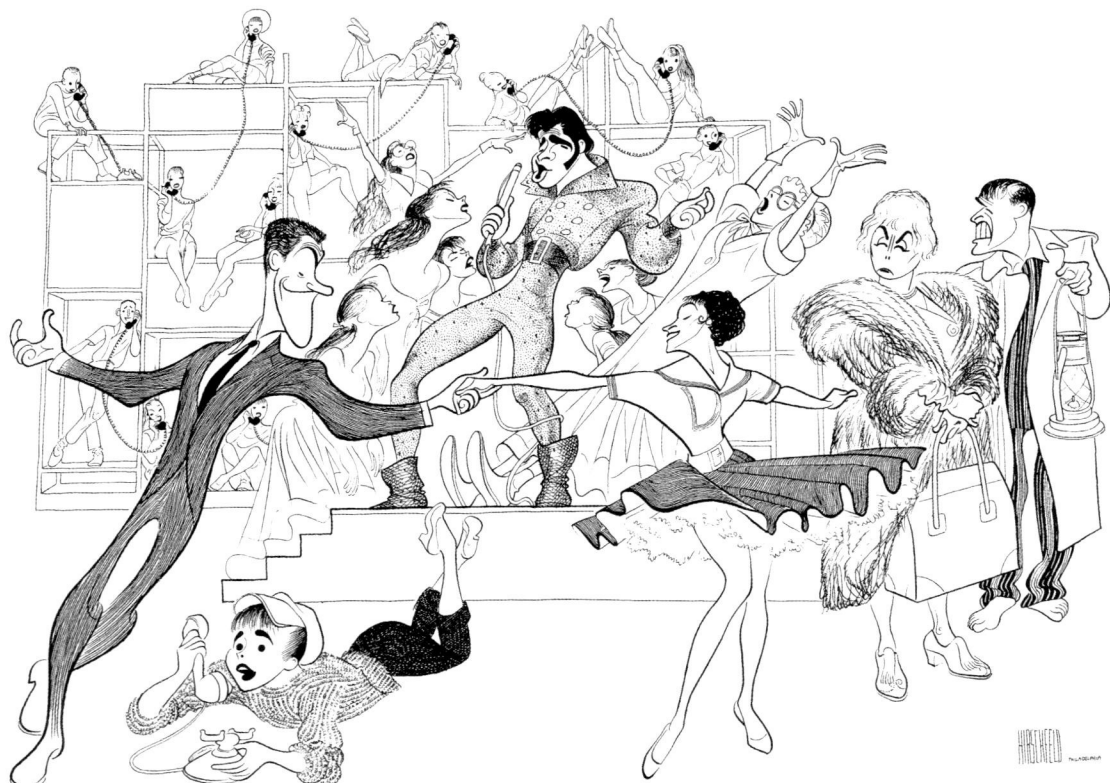

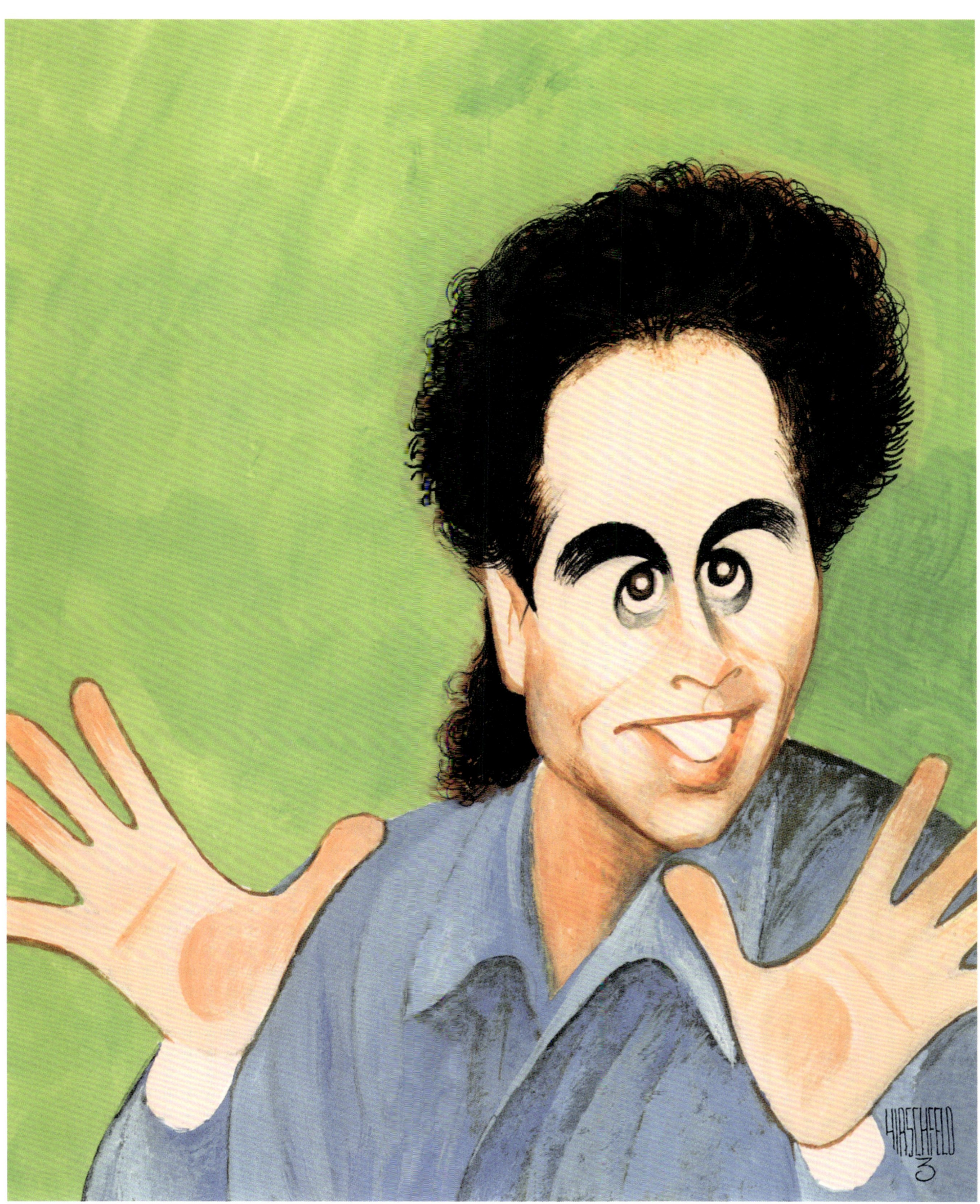

JERRY SEINFELD

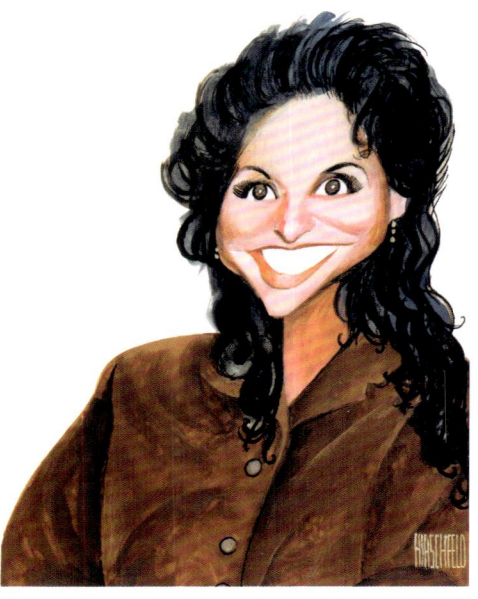

b. April 29, 1954

Gouache on board, 1998

TV Guide cover, March 2, 1998

How did a show that boasted it was about "nothing" become one of the most popular television programs of all time? The same reason that Hirschfeld enjoyed watching it: The characters were relatable. Jerry Seinfeld, Larry David, and their writers, as well as the actors themselves, created characters whom viewers felt they knew in real life. Jerry, Elaine (Julia Louis-Dreyfus), George (Jason Alexander), and Kramer (Michael Richards) are all like Hirschfeld drawings—they are caricatures, but rooted in reality. Their exaggerations do not distort them—OK, maybe Kramer is a bit distorted—but rather, their artificiality heightens the reality of the show.

In 1994, Larry David commissioned a drawing of Seinfeld and himself working at their partner desk (this work can occasionally be seen in the background of *Curb Your Enthusiasm*). It took *The New York Times* for Hirschfeld to get an assignment to draw the full cast. This image proved to be so popular it was published as a hand-signed limited-edition print. The following year, a collector asked for a different image of the cast, and that too was published as a print.

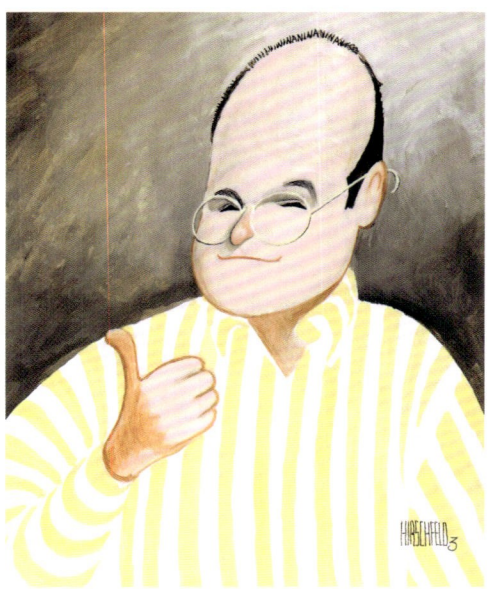

The show debuted in 1989, but the "Gab Four," as Hirschfeld liked to call them, reached icon status in 1998, when *TV Guide* asked for individual portraits of each of the leads and published the same issue with four different covers for their May 9–15 issue. Their images were instantly recognizable to audiences, and the success of the four-cover gambit confirmed their status as pop-culture avatars.

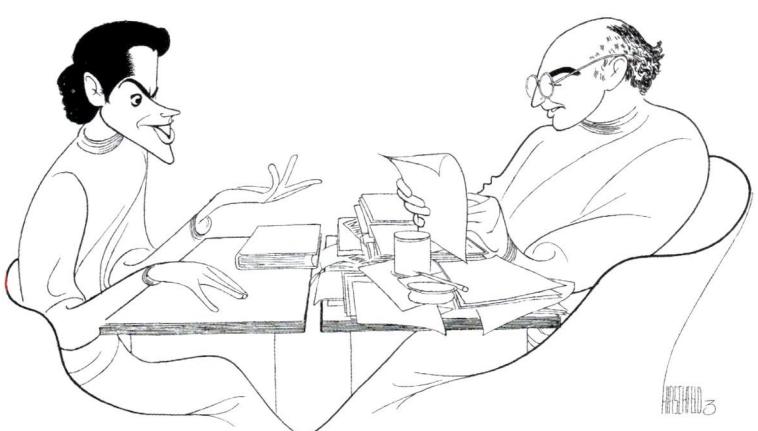

ABOVE

Jerry Seinfeld and Larry David, 1994

RIGHT, TOP TO BOTTOM

A series of *TV Guide* covers featuring Elaine (Julia Louis-Dreyfus), George (Jason Alexander), and Kramer (Michael Richards), 1998

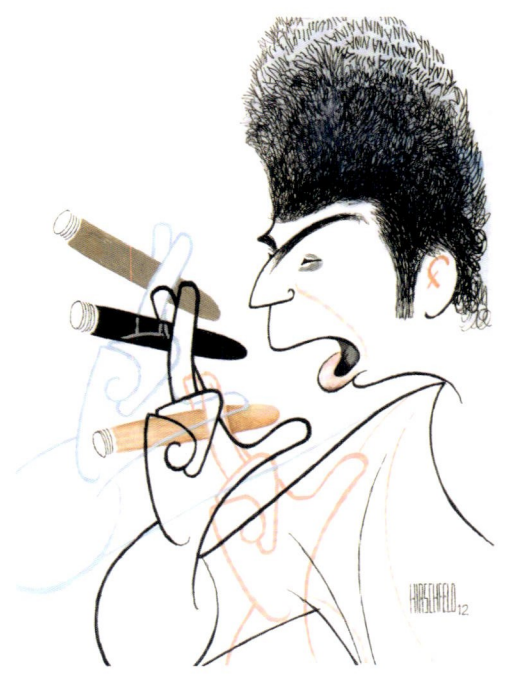

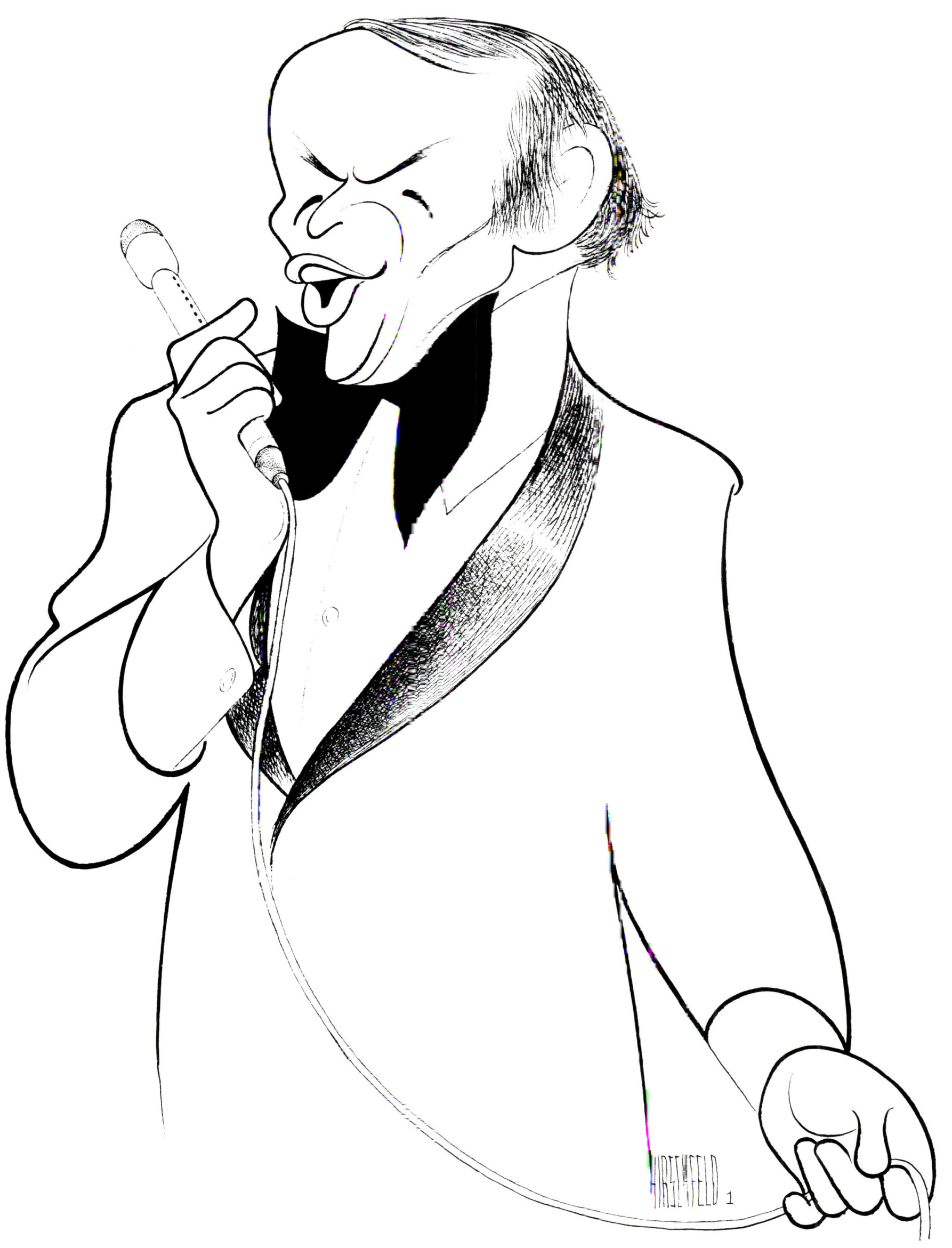

FRANK SINATRA

December 12, 1915–May 14, 1998

Ink on board, 1974

The New York Times, October 13, 1974

In 1991, the legendary Friars Club honored Hirschfeld with a special evening. Frank Sinatra could not be there, but he sent a note saying that no one captured the energy of New York City better than Hirschfeld, especially during the 1940s and '50s. Sinatra would know—his career, which began in the 1940s in New York, was immortalized by Hirschfeld at that time. His first drawing of Sinatra appeared in 1944 in an advertisement for the singer's show on CBS Radio. Over the next fifty-eight years, Hirschfeld charted Sinatra's rise from popular singer to acclaimed actor to performing legend and finally American icon, in more than fifty images that promoted his concerts, films, and TV specials. Sinatra liked the illustrations so much that he acquired a number of drawings for his personal collection.

In 1974, Sinatra performed a record-setting six nights at New York's Madison Square Garden, accompanied by his own band and augmented by Woody Herman's Thundering Herd and a string section. The stage was set up like a boxing ring—the Garden hosted regular boxing matches—and sportscaster Howard Cosell was the emcee each evening. The final night of the run was broadcast on television the day this drawing appeared in *The New York Times*. The show was later released as a live album and subsequently included in a box set of Sinatra's live recordings. Sinatra was the only singer of his generation who could have pulled off such a spectacular series of sold-out shows at one of America's largest indoor venues. And who better to commemorate them than Hirschfeld?

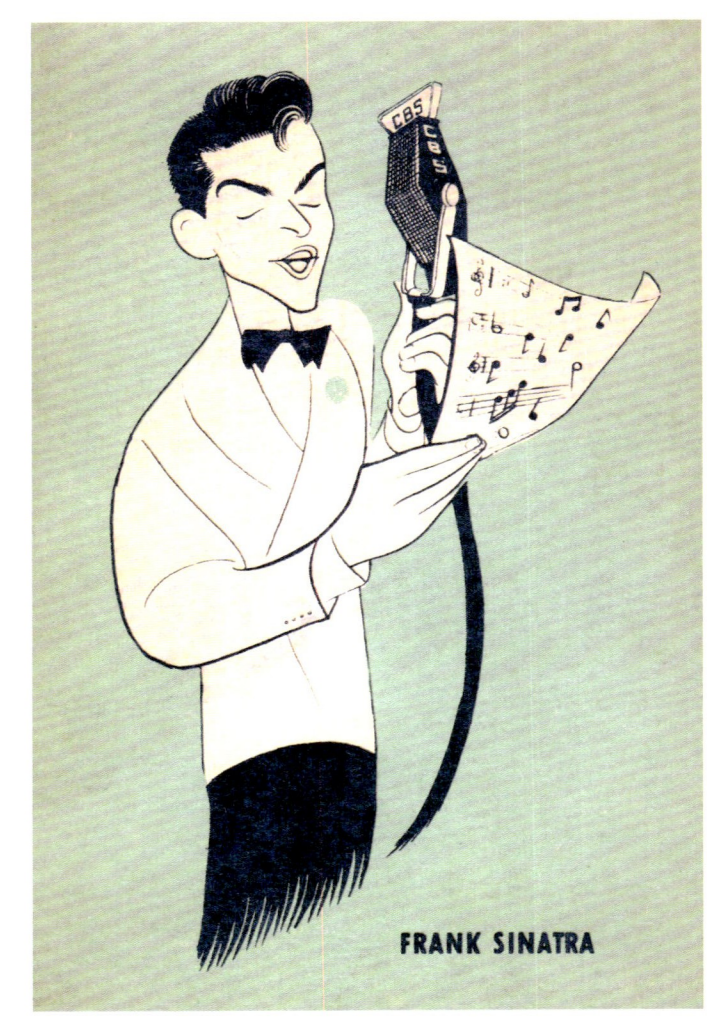

FRANK SINATRA

TOP
CBS Radio postcard of Frank Sinatra, 1944

RIGHT
Anchors Aweigh, 1945
LEFT TO RIGHT: Frank Sinatra, Kathryn Grayson, and Gene Kelly

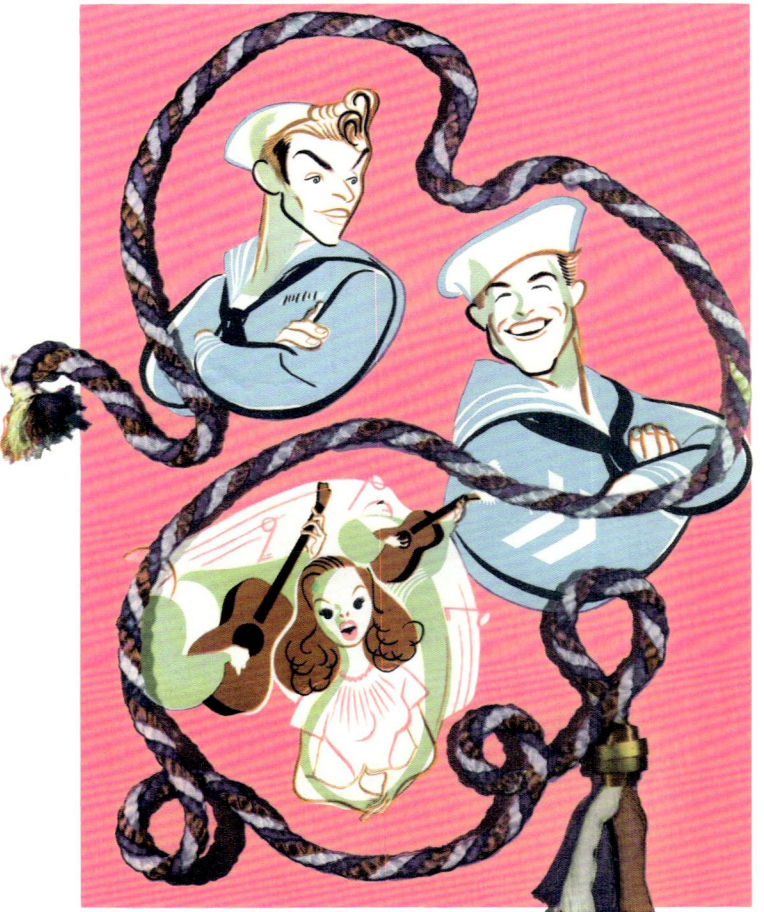

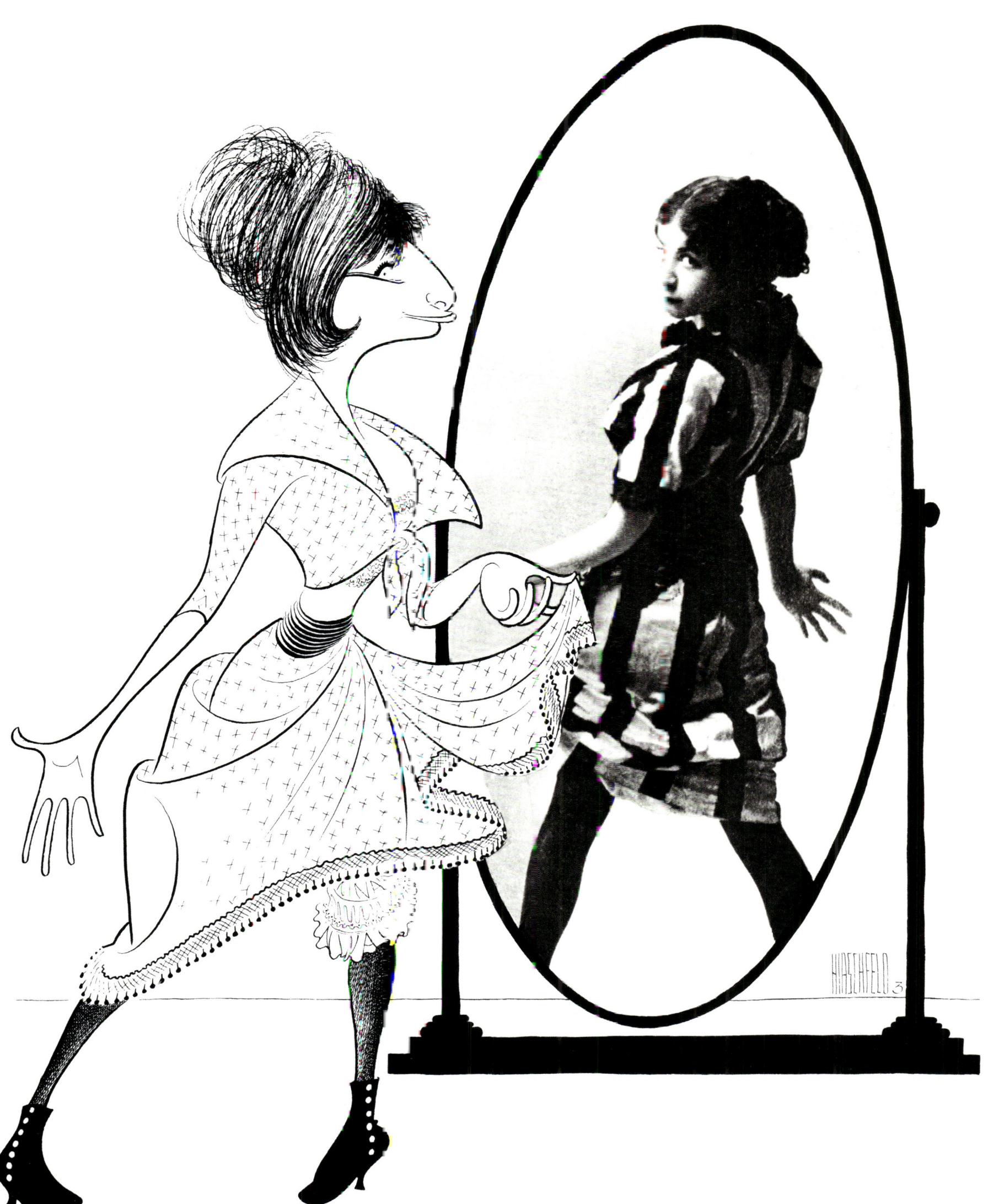

BARBRA STREISAND

b. April 24, 1942

Ink and collaged photograph on board, 1964

The New York Times, March 22, 1964

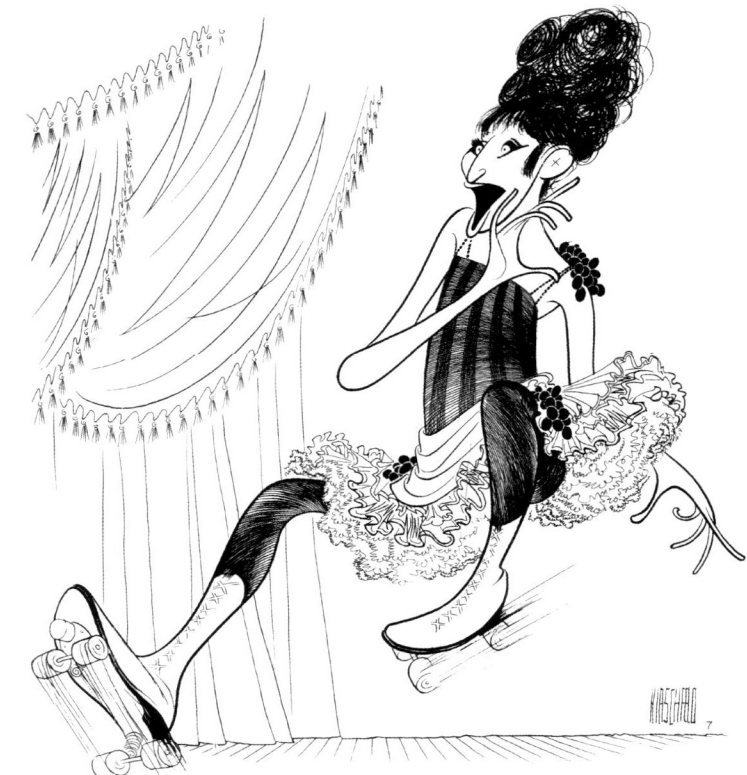

With a career spanning more than sixty years, Barbra Streisand has achieved so much success across multiple fields of entertainment that she was one of the first EGOTs, winning Emmy, Grammy, Oscar, and Tony awards. She has had historic performances on Broadway; has written, directed, produced, and starred in major Hollywood hits; has created television specials that had millions of viewers; and is the only recording artist to have had a number one album in each of the last six decades.

Hirschfeld drew all of it. He was at Streisand's audition for her first Broadway musical, *I Can Get It for You Wholesale*, and sketched its out-of-town tryouts in Boston in 1962. He captured her in her career-defining Broadway role in *Funny Girl* in this drawing from March 1964—a rare newspaper photo collage showing the hand-drawn Streisand before a mirror incorporating a 1910 photo of Fanny Brice, whom she played in the Jule Styne musical. Hirschfeld also recorded her budding TV-movie career in 1967 in the vaudeville-era pastiche *The Belle of 14th Street*. When she made her first film in 1968, an adaptation of the stage musical *Funny Girl*, Hirschfeld depicted her in the made-for-the-film song "Roller Skate Rag."

In 1969, Streisand formed the First Artists production company with Paul Newman and Sidney Poitier, who were later joined by Steve McQueen and Dustin Hoffman. When all the stars were on board, the company was announced with a Hirschfeld drawing.

As Streisand concentrated almost exclusively on film for much of the 1970s, Hirschfeld drew five of them from the decade, including *What's Up, Doc?* and *The Way We Were*, some for the *Times* and others to promote the films themselves. In 1993, she released her *Back to Broadway* album and had Sony commission a Hirschfeld drawing to celebrate it. The same year, *The New York Times* wrote that Streisand "enjoys a cultural status that only one other American entertainer, Frank Sinatra, has achieved in the last half century." Like Sinatra, Streisand understood Hirschfeld's genius at capturing the vitality of their performances. It takes an icon to recognize another.

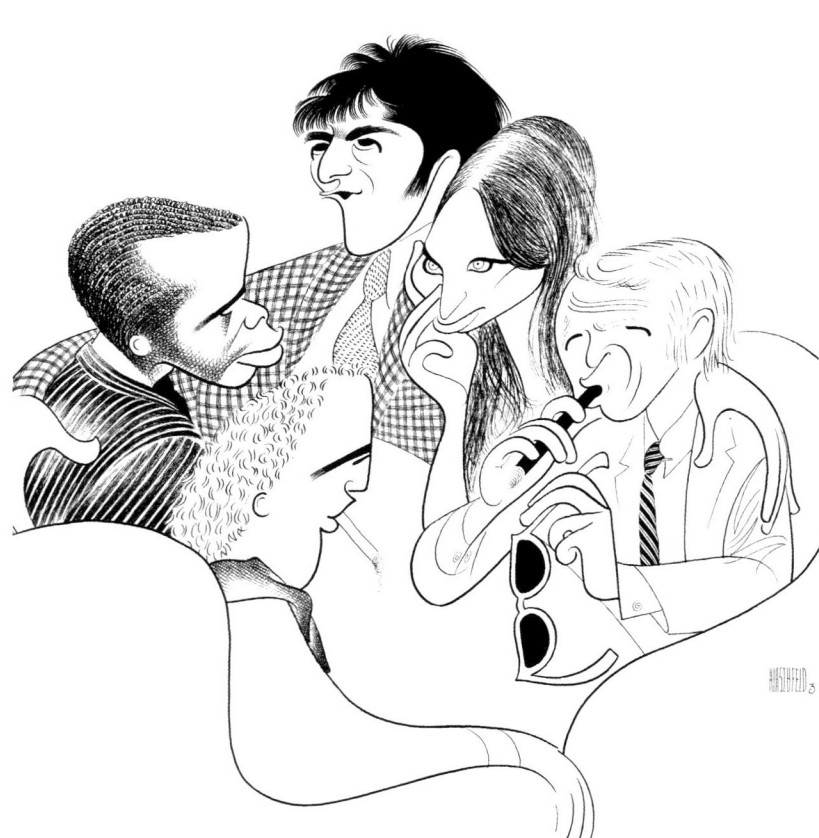

ABOVE

Funny Girl, 1968

A scene from the film adaptation of the Broadway musical

LEFT

The Big Five at First Artists Productions, 1972

CLOCKWISE FROM LEFT: Sidney Poitier, Dustin Hoffman, Barbra Streisand, Steve McQueen, and Paul Newman

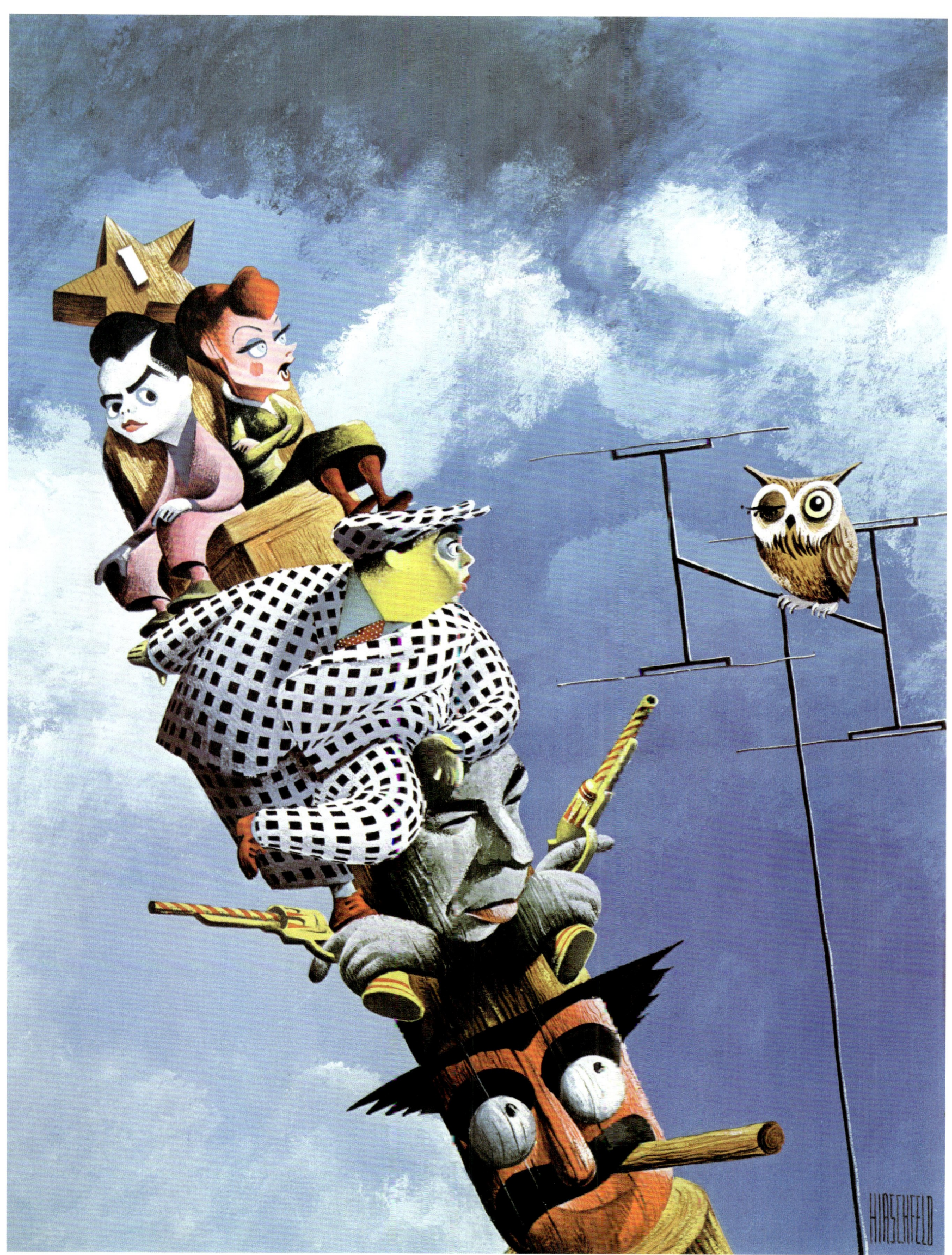

TV TOTEM POLE

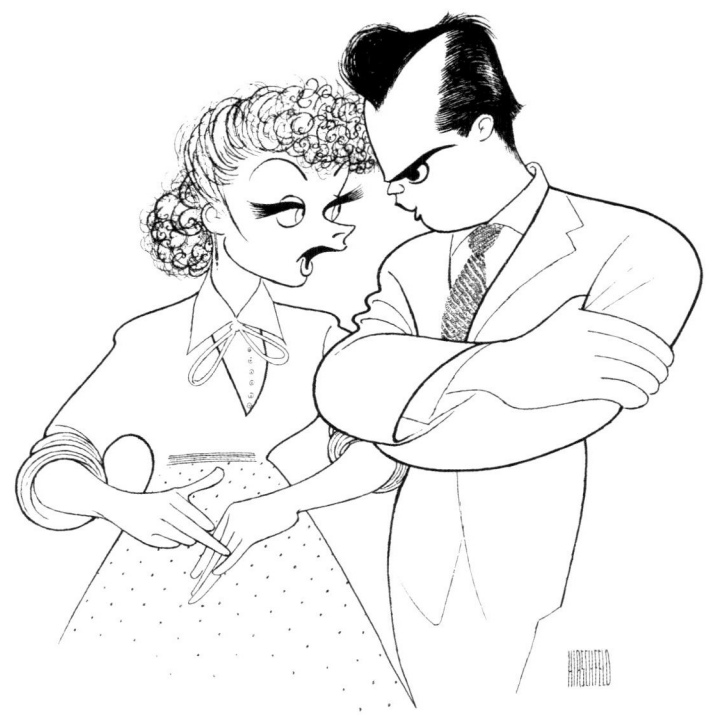

From top left to bottom: Desi Arnaz, Lucille Ball, Jackie Gleason, Jack Webb, and Groucho Marx

Gouache and ink on board, 1954

Collier's cover, October 29, 1954

In 1954, television was a new but quickly growing entertainment option for households across the United States. That year, the top-rated shows were, in order: *I Love Lucy*, *The Jackie Gleason Show*, Jack Webb's *Dragnet*, and *You Bet Your Life* hosted by Groucho Marx. Hirschfeld took this information and combined it with the country's embrace of frontier America in the post-war boom—which had been co-opting the totem pole and other Indigenous iconography in various media—to create this striking cover for *Collier's*, one of the most popular weekly magazines in mid-century America. With a limited number of shows on TV in this period, these weekly performances had an extraordinary hold of the country's attention. Hirschfeld literally made them icons with this image.

To this day, these four shows continue to resonate with audiences all over the world. *I Love Lucy* has been on the air virtually every day since the end of its six-season run in 1957.

The Jackie Gleason Show spawned *The Honeymooners*, whose enduring popularity was the inspiration for other television shows, most notably *The Flintstones*. In just thirty-nine classic episodes, the show also introduced memorable catchphrases into American culture, such as "Bang, zoom, straight to the moon!" "Homina homina homina," and "Baby, you're the greatest."

Dragnet's seven-year television run was the first in the *Dragnet* media franchise that eventually encompassed film, books, and comics. The show's distinct four-note introduction is instantly recognizable.

And Groucho showed that he did not need a greasepaint mustache or any of his brothers to amuse and delight audiences. His ad-libs are legendary, and the show's catchphrase, "Say the secret word . . . ," has taken on a life of its own outside of the program, which started on radio in 1947 and moved to television from 1950 to 1961, making him an even more iconic comedian than he already was.

Perhaps Hirschfeld was clairvoyant, as situation comedies, crime dramas, and game shows—which were pioneered by the performers in this image—essentially created the template for television for the next several decades.

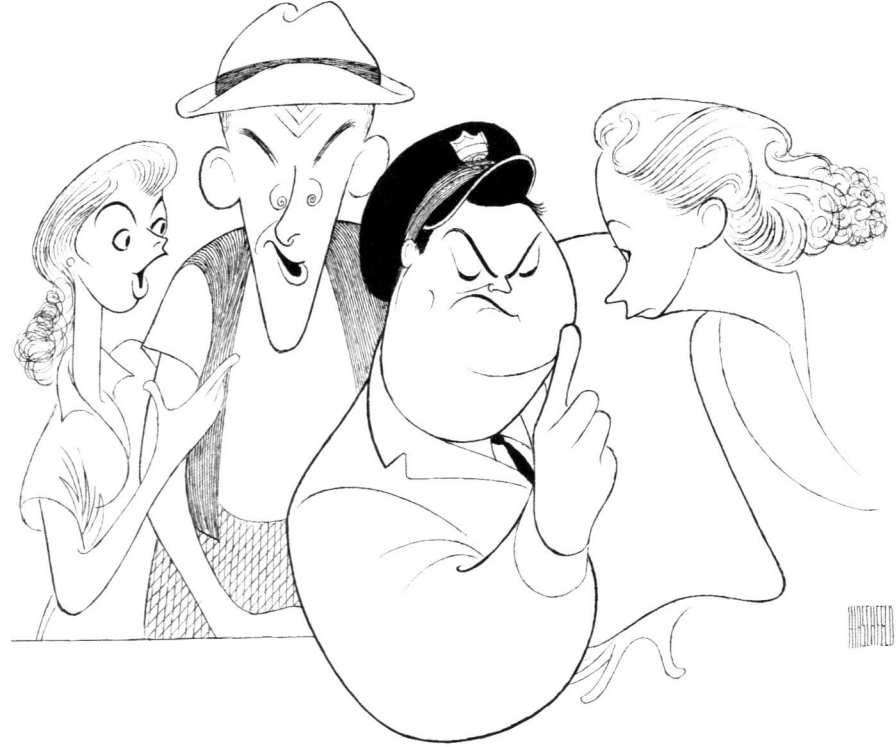

ABOVE
I Love Lucy, 1989
Lucille Ball and Desi Arnaz from a limited-edition etching

LEFT
The Honeymooners, 1985
Joyce Randolph, Art Carney, Jackie Gleason, and Audrey Meadows